EASY LACE
Knits

EASY LACE
Knits

All You Need to Know to Start Knitting Lace &
20 Simply Beautiful Patterns

ANNIKEN ALLIS

STACKPOLE
BOOKS

Guilford, Connecticut

Stackpole Books
An imprint of The Rowman & Littlefield Publishing Group, Inc.
4501 Forbes Blvd., Ste. 200, Lanham, MD 20706

Distributed by NATIONAL BOOK NETWORK
800-462-6420

Model photography by Gale Zucker
Technique photography by Rob Frost

We have made every effort to ensure the accuracy and completeness of these instructions. We cannot, however, be responsible for human error, typographical mistakes, or variations in individual work.

British Library Cataloguing in Publication Information Available

Library of Congress Cataloging-in-Publication Data

Names: Allis, Anniken, author.
Title: Easy lace knits : all you need to know to start knitting lace & 20
  simply beautiful patterns / Anniken Allis.
Description: Guilford, Connecticut : Stackpole Books, 2018. | Includes index.
  Identifiers: LCCN 2018016717 (print) | LCCN 2018017640 (ebook) | ISBN
  9780811767552 (e-book) | ISBN 9780811719018 (pbk. : alk. paper)
Subjects: LCSH: Knitted laces—Patterns.
Classification: LCC TT805.K54 (ebook) | LCC TT805.K54 A45 2018 (print) | DDC
  746.2/26—dc23
LC record available at https://lccn.loc.gov/2018016717

♾™ The paper used in this publication meets the minimum requirements of American National Standard for Information Sciences—Permanence of Paper for Printed Library Materials, ANSI/NISO Z39.48-1992.

First edition

Printed in the United States of America

Contents

Introduction

In 2006 I was given a beautiful lace book for Christmas, and that was the start of my lace knitting journey. I had been trying to teach myself how to knit lace with the help of a big knitting reference book and online videos. Once I'd worked out how to make a yarn over, the world of lace opened up to me. The lace book I was given had lots of stunning patterns, and even though my lace knitting skills were fairly basic, I jumped in, choosing two of the shawls. They weren't easy to make, but I learned so much by working through them.

The only way we learn and develop is by doing and by challenging ourselves. In *Easy Lace Knits*, I've given you the tools to conquer lace knitting. There are lots of detailed close-ups of all the techniques you need, as well as advice on how to make lace knitting easier and how to read my knitting patterns and/or charts.

The patterns are arranged by order of difficulty. If you are new to lace knitting, I recommend starting with one of the easier patterns and working your way through the book, gradually choosing more difficult patterns. This will build your confidence and skills.

Lace patterns look much more difficult than they are. Knitting is only a combination of knit and purl stitches, and lace knitting has a few yarn overs and decreases thrown in. Just take it one stitch at a time. Read the advice on using stitch markers and lifelines, and cast on. Knit swatches to practice the lace stitches before you start a project. I also recommend that you practice unpicking lace stitches and fixing mistakes. Keep practicing! It doesn't matter if you make a mistake; you can rip out your knitting and use the yarn again. Just think of it as better value for your money.

As your confidence grows, move on to more difficult patterns. Soon you'll be wowing your friends with complicated lace shawls and garments.

And remember, knitting should be fun and relaxing, so if you're not enjoying a project, rip it out and find another one. Don't let mistakes slow you down. Remember, it's only knitting. Unpick, fix your mistake, and carry on.

If you find it difficult to learn the techniques from the photos and instructions, search online for video tutorials. My website, yarnaddict.co.uk, has a long list of tutorials, and I regularly post new ones. You can also find me on Instagram, Twitter, and Ravelry as YarnAddictAnni. The Love of Lace Knitting Facebook group is full of knitters who love lace knitting, and there is always room for one more.

I hope this book will make you fall in love with lace knitting, like I did. I hope you enjoy this book as much as I enjoyed creating it. I love your feedback, so please do get in touch.

Happy knitting!
Anniken

Making Lace Knitting Easier

If you're new to lace knitting, this book will walk you through the stitches and skills you need to know and give you 20 patterns to test your skills on. You probably already know many, if not all, of the stitches used in this book; it's the combination of them that makes "lace." If you've already dipped your toe into the lace-knitting pond, then it's probably the gorgeous shawls and sweaters that inspired you to pick up this book, and you can skip right ahead to those, referring to the techniques section only as needed.

Patterns are arranged into three levels of difficulty: Level 1 is the easiest, 3 is the most difficult. It is hard to divide patterns into degrees of difficulty because it's all relative. How challenging a technique is depends on your level of experience. If you know how to knit, purl, cast on, and bind off, and can follow a pattern (see How to Read a Pattern on this page if you're unsure), then you will be able to knit the patterns in this book.

Since lace knitting comes with some extra challenges, I've outlined some tricks of the lace-knitting trade in this chapter. You'll find helpful information on how to prevent and fix mistakes, how to choose yarn, and how to plan ahead to ensure success, among other useful bits of knowledge, such as understanding basic shawl shaping.

Remember, knitting is supposed to be fun! But you will develop your skills only if you challenge yourself to try more difficult patterns. If you knit plain garter stitch scarves every time, you will never improve or learn new stitches and techniques. Look at each pattern as a learning opportunity, and don't be afraid of making mistakes. We learn more from those errors than we do from getting everything right the first time.

Knitting a pattern you think is more difficult than what you've knitted before really boosts your confidence and gives you a huge sense of pride and satisfaction when you finish it, so don't be afraid to try any of the patterns in this book. If you're unsure of a technique or stitch pattern, practice on a swatch first. Use lifelines and stitch markers as described in this chapter to keep your place in the pattern and to help you correct mistakes. And, remember, this is only knitting; it's supposed to be fun—it's not a matter of life or death. If you make a mistake, rip it out and start again. I know it's frustrating, but it's better than giving up. Take the instructions one step at a time. If you're not sure you understand what you're being asked to do, just try following the instructions. Practice on a swatch and actually do what the pattern says, step by step. Many things make more sense when you're actually knitting than just reading about it.

If you don't feel ready to dive into the patterns yet, knit some practice swatches. Look through the book, find a stitch pattern you like, and knit a practice square or even a mini shawl. Knit a few swatches from different stitch patterns.

During my workshops, I've noticed that most knitters are actually better than they think they are. Usually it's a question of confidence and being willing to give it a go. We can all learn new things, and we can all improve. Whether you've been knitting for a few months or 70 years, you can knit the patterns in this book. I think your attitude is more important than your experience. If you're willing to give new techniques a go and aren't worried about making mistakes, you will learn much more quickly and enjoy your knitting much more than if you're nervous of trying new things.

How to Read a Pattern

Every designer has a slightly different way of writing patterns, and every publisher and magazine have a slightly different pattern style. This can make reading patterns somewhat confusing. These days, you can easily purchase patterns, books, and magazines online from anywhere in the world, and different countries have different styles of writing patterns. In some countries, the norm is to include a lot of information and step-by-step instructions; in other countries, patterns are very brief.

When you knit a pattern from new designers, it can take some adjustment to follow their patterns as you have to learn their individual "language" and how they structure their patterns.

Here, I'm going to explain how to find your way through one of my patterns.

Yarn Requirements, Measurements, and Gauge

At the beginning of a pattern, you will find yarn requirements, details about which needle size to use, other notions needed, measurements, and details about gauge. Remember, you will only achieve the measurements stated if you knit to the correct gauge and block the garment correctly (I have a free online blocking tutorial; see my website for details).

If you're knitting a shawl or a scarf where fit is not as important, you can worry less about getting the exact gauge, although a difference in gauge won't just affect finished size, it will affect how much yarn you need, too. Please bear this in mind if your gauge varies from the pattern.

Difficulty Level

I've added difficulty levels to the patterns in this book and listed the stitches and techniques used in each pattern to give you a quick idea on what skills you will need for every piece. It's always difficult to assign a difficulty level—I don't want to discourage you from trying any pattern in this book! Basically, though, Level 1 patterns have simple shapes and easy lace patterns, while higher levels have more complicated shapes and more difficult lace patterns.

Special Stitches and Techniques

This section will give basic instructions for any stitches or techniques that are less common, which you can refer to as you work the pattern.

Notes

Always check the notes! They will give an overview of the construction of the piece and draw your attention to any tricky points in the pattern or things to keep in mind as you work.

Charts

I love knitting from charts, but I know not all of you do, so I always include written instructions for each chart. Refer to the chart key to see what stitch each symbol represents. See page 4 for more on how to read charts.

The Pattern

If I want you to use a specific cast-on method, I will tell you in the pattern. If there is no cast-on method listed, you can use your preferred method.

I include frequent stitch counts and stitches increased or decreased in my patterns. At the end of a row on which you are increasing or decreasing and at other key points in the pattern, you will find the stitch count in italics.

Charts are an integral part of the pattern, and the instructions for how and when to use them are included as part of the pattern. The written instructions for each chart are included after the main pattern text. In some cases, only right-side rows are charted; the wrong-side row instructions will be given in the pattern and the written instructions for the chart.

At the end of the pattern, I will tell you which bind-off to use if there's a reason for using a specific one. Most of the time you will want to use a stretchy bind-off for lace knitting, but there may be exceptions. If no bind-off is listed, then you can use whichever method you prefer.

Finishing

You will find instructions for what to do once you've finished all the knitting. If it's a shawl or scarf, it will simply tell you to weave in all the loose ends and block the piece. If you're making a garment where there's sewing up to do, the pattern will give you the order for doing that.

Yarn Substitutions

Many knitters worry about substituting yarn, but it's easier than you think. Just follow a few simple rules.

First, look at the fiber content of the yarn used in the original pattern. There may be a reason why the designer has chosen a specific fiber or combination of fibers, so for successful yarn substitution it is important to take fiber content into account. You may wish to use an alternative fiber, but before you decide, take into account how that fiber behaves and how it will look in the chosen stitch pattern. For example, a lace pattern knitted in smooth silk will appear very different from the same swatch knitted in brushed mohair, as the fluffy mohair will fill in some of the holes in the lace.

Also look at the yards per skein. You want to use a yarn that is about the same thickness as the original yarn, and matching this ratio will help to ensure that. If the yarn specified has 400 yards/366 meters in a 3.5-ounce/100-gram skein, choose a yarn that has the same number of yards in the same size skein (or the same ratio of yards/meters to ounces/grams in a different size skein).

Always knit a swatch in your new yarn to make sure it works well with the needle size and stitch pattern. And don't forget to check your gauge. Your new yarn may knit up to a different gauge than the pattern's original yarn.

In accessories such as shawls and scarves that don't need to have an exact fit, substituting yarn is relatively simple. I recommend knitting a swatch to make sure you are happy with the new yarn and needle size combination. Always block lace before making a decision on whether or not you like the resulting fabric.

You may also want to purposely choose a yarn in a different weight to achieve a different effect from the same stitch pattern. For example, a square or circular shawl can be knitted in lace-weight yarn, but if you choose a worsted-weight yarn, it will become a warm afghan instead of a delicate shawl. Keep in mind that if you choose to knit the item in a different yarn weight, you may need more yardage than the pattern states.

Swatching: It's about More than Gauge

Many knitters ignore swatching, thinking it's a waste of time, but it's actually a very important part of knitting a pattern. Swatching will tell you many things about your chosen project.

First, it's important to knit a swatch to check your gauge. Before you start your swatch, check which stitch pattern the swatch is knitted in. Make a note of the measurements of your swatch before you block it (for reference on if or how much the gauge changes with blocking), but always wash and block a swatch before measuring the gauge you are matching for the pattern. For garments, gauge is important for a good fit. If your gauge is off, then the garment won't be the size you planned for. I like to double-check my gauge as I knit garments. After knitting a few inches on the back, I will measure the width and double-check it against the measurements in the pattern to make sure I'm still on track, taking into account any variance I found from my pre- and post-blocked swatch.

Swatching will also tell you if you like the yarn you've chosen, and if it works with the stitch pattern used in the pattern. If you're unsure of a specific yarn, get a small amount (like one ball) and knit a swatch before you go ahead and buy the full amount needed for the project.

If the project includes techniques that are new to you, it's a good idea to practice them on a swatch first. This will help you iron out any problems before you start on the actual project.

Many knitters think that gauge doesn't matter when it comes to accessories like shawls and scarves, and they're partly right. The main problem with not getting gauge is that you may use more yarn than the pattern states. So if you decide to throw caution to the wind and not swatch, then do make sure you have more yarn available. Not knitting to the correct gauge will also affect the final size of the item.

Reading Charts

These are things you should know about knitting charts:

- Charts are a visual representation of your knitting and show what your knitting will look like when you see it from the right side.
- Each square on a chart represents one stitch.
- Charts are read from bottom to top.
- Right-side rows—normally odd-numbered rows—are read from right to left and will have the row number on the right side of the chart.
- Wrong-side rows—normally even-numbered rows—are read from left to right and will have the row number on the left side of the chart.
- When knitting in the round, all rows/rounds face the right side as you knit, and all round numbers will be on the right side of the chart.
- On many lace patterns, every other row is a "rest" row, which means it's a plain knit or a plain purl row, perhaps with edging stitches. These easy repetitive rows are quite often taken out of the chart, and the instructions are given only in the pattern. This means that only right-side rows are charted, and the pattern will alert you to this.
- All charts have a key, or legend, that will tell you what the different symbols mean. Unfortunately, there is no international standard system for knitting chart symbols, so always check the key before you knit.
- Sections of the chart that are repeated (known as "pattern repeats") are shown inside red borders on the chart and in brackets [ ] in the written instructions.

Using a Lifeline

If you make a mistake in lace knitting, it can be difficult to unknit or rip out your work without losing track of the yarn overs, which disappear quickly into the surrounding stitches. A lifeline is the solution to this problem. It is simply a piece of waste yarn that holds live stitches from a row that you know is correct as you continue to knit onward. Then, if you make a mistake and need to unravel several rows, you can take your needles out and unravel down to the lifeline, where your stitches are held safely. Simply run your needle through the stitches, following the path of the lifeline,

to place them back on your needle, ready to continue knitting. Remove the lifeline and reinsert it after several rows of error-free knitting. Lifelines can be inserted at the end of each pattern repeat or every 10 or 20 rows, for example. It can also be useful to insert a lifeline if you're starting another section of the pattern or starting a shaping section.

1. To insert a lifeline, take a piece of smooth yarn slightly thinner or the same thickness as your working yarn (for lace-weight yarn, I recommend using a smooth fingering-weight yarn) and, using a blunt tapestry needle, thread the yarn through all your stitches while leaving them on the needle. If you are using a circular needle, push all the stitches onto the cable and you will have more space to thread the tapestry needle through. Secure the waste yarn by tying the ends together.

2. Continue knitting.

Stitch Markers

Stitch markers are great tools for keeping track of where you are in your pattern to help you find and correct mistakes. For example, imagine you are knitting a row of 100 stitches with a pattern repeat of 10 stitches. If you finish the row and only have 99 stitches, trying to find the mistake can be difficult. But, if you placed a stitch marker between each pattern repeat (that is, every 10 stitches), you can count the stitches between each marker and you'll easily find the pattern repeat with only 9 stitches. Then you can go through the stitches in that pattern repeat to find your error.

I recommend smooth ring markers for lace knitting. Handmade or fancy stitch markers can get tangled up in your delicate yarn. A length of waste yarn tied in a loop can also be used as a stitch marker. Place stitch markers between each pattern repeat, to mark off edgings or center stitches, and to help with shaping.

When stitch markers are positioned next to yarn overs, they can sometimes slip through to the other side of the yarn over and end up in the wrong place. Watch out for this, especially when using stitch markers to mark a center spine stitch (as in a triangular top-down shawl). A locking stitch marker placed right on the stitch can be helpful in this instance; just move it up every few rows.

Reading Your Knitting

I strongly recommend that you look at your knitting as you work the various decreases and yarn overs and pay attention to what the different stitches look like as they come off your needles. It will help you to learn to "read" your knitting and identify errors and correct mistakes easier. The only way to learn to read your knitting is to practice looking at what happens below your needles when you work various stitches.

Learning to read your knitting will also help you to knit without being as dependent on the chart. I often look at charts and make a mental note of the shape of the lace pattern, and then I can frequently knit it without referring to the chart for every stitch. I don't necessarily memorize the stitch pattern; I just notice the shapes, and, together with my lace knitting knowledge and recognizing how different decreases look, I can knit patterns without constantly referring to the chart. Of course it takes time to get to that point, but most of the patterns in this book have some easy-to-learn repeats that will help you in this area.

Here's how to improve your knit-reading ability:
- Look at what happens when you work various stitches. Notice what they look like immediately after you've worked them and what they look like a few rows later.
- Notice which shapes are emerging on your needles and how these shapes relate to the chart you're knitting from.
- Learn to read lace charts. This will help you to see shapes and to look at the lace pattern as a whole rather than just individual stitches.
- Practice! Anything worth learning takes practice. We all learn at different rates. If you struggle, just keep practicing. You'll get better if you keep challenging yourself.

Fixing Mistakes

If you're new to lace knitting, it can be difficult to fix mistakes. I strongly recommend inserting regular lifelines (see Using a Lifeline, page 4), which make it easy to rip back to a place where your knitting was correct.

But there are a few mistakes that can be easily fixed without ripping. The easiest mistakes to fix are forgotten or dropped yarn overs on the previous row. On the first row after the missed yarn over, work to the point where the yarn over should have been, pick up the strand between the two stitches and place it on your left needle, then knit or purl it as directed in the pattern. If you are on the second row after the missed yarn over, work to the point where the yarn over should be, and then pick up the second strand down and, using a crochet hook or your knitting needle, loop the top strand through it.

The best way to learn to fix mistakes is to knit some squares and deliberately make some mistakes. It's always best to practice before you have to do it on a real project.

The most important skill in learning to fix mistakes is to be able to read your knitting so you can recognize what various stitches look like. This will help you to spot mistakes sooner, and to know whether or not you have actually made a mistake.

I have several videos for fixing a variety of lace knitting mistakes on my website, so check those out for more visual help on this topic. It's much easier to learn through video than with words and photos.

How to Work Various Shawl Shapes

Shawls are definitely a favorite when it comes to lace knitting, and understanding the basics of how different shapes are constructed can help you to see how a pattern is working as you knit it. Some shawl shapes can be a bit confusing the first time you make them, so here I've covered a few shapes to help you better recognize what you're doing. Watch what happens on your needles as you knit. See which shape emerges. It will help you understand and read your knitting better.

Valencia, Napoli, St. Tropez, Palma, and Ibiza are all shawls that are worked from the top down in a similar way, even though they are different shapes. They all have increases worked on either side of one or two spines and at the beginning and end of every other row, which is how the shape is achieved.

Triangle

VALENCIA

Let's look at Valencia (page 87) first. Here's the first part of the pattern, after you've cast on 9 stitches:

Row 1 (RS): Sl wyif, k2, (yo, k1) three times, yo, k3. *4 sts inc.*

Row 2 (WS and all following WS rows): Sl wyif, k2, p to last 3 sts, k3.

Row 3: Sl wyif, k2, yo, k3, yo, **k1**, yo, k3, yo, k3. *4 sts inc.*

I recommend placing a locking stitch marker on the stitch in bold. This will become the central spine stitch. Move the marker up every few rows.

Row 5: Sl wyif, k2, yo, k to marked st, yo, **k1**, yo, k to last 3 sts, yo, k3. *4 sts inc.*

Continue as established, increasing 4 stitches every other row.

In this pattern, you are increasing by working a yarn over after the first 3 stitches, either side of a central spine, and before the last 3 stitches. Together, these four increases on every right-side row create the triangular shape.

It's easier to knit a shawl like this on a circular needle (although you can start on straight needles, if preferred). The advantage of a circular needle is that you can see the shape emerging. Push all your stitches onto the cable part of the needle, and stretch your knitting out so you can see the shape clearly. It will also be easier to fit in all the stitches as you gradually increase.

On Row 3, you will establish the shaping, and it's important to get this row correct. A triangle like Valencia is actually two triangles separated by a center spine to make a larger triangle. I find it easier to remember to increase on either side of the central spine if I put a removable marker on the spine stitch. You can get plastic markers that look like small padlocks. These are perfect, as they're light and you can easily attach and remove them from stitches.

Many knitters use ring markers, which you place on your needles between 2 stitches. You can put one of these markers in front of the spine stitch to help you remember to increase. But *please note:* If you put a ring marker next to a yarn over, it may slip through the yarn over and end up in the wrong place. Using the padlock stitch markers attached to the spine stitch avoids this problem, but you will have to remember to move it up every few rows.

If you look at the pattern, you will see that on Row 3 you knit 3 stitches between the yarn overs. On Row 5, you knit 5 stitches between the yarn overs. Each time you work another right-side row, the number of stitches between the yarn overs in each half of the triangular shawl increases by 2 stitches. The k1 in bold is the spine stitch.

> **Row 3:** Sl wyif, k2, yo, **k3**, yo, **k1**, yo, **k3**, yo, k3.
> *4 sts inc.*
> **Row 5:** Sl wyif, k2, yo, **k5**, yo, **k1**, yo, **k5**, yo, k3.
> *4 sts inc.*

Working the Chart

Let's stay with Valencia and look at Chart A. After you finish the stockinette stitch section, you have 129 stitches, which are broken down like this:

- 3 stitches at the beginning of the row for the garter stitch edging
- 61 stitches for the first triangle
- 1 stitch for the center spine
- 61 stitches for the second triangle
- 3 stitches for the garter stitch edging at the end of the row

Chart A will be worked over the 61 stitches in each triangle. If I were to chart out the full width of the shawl, Chart A would look like the chart on the left.

This takes up a lot of space, and, if you look closely, you will see that the first section between the first 3 stitches and the spine is identical to the section between the spine and the last 3 stitches. So in my patterns I take out the edging stitches (in this shawl, that's 3 stitches at the beginning and at the end of each row) and the spine stitches. I then take one section out and put it in a separate chart like the one on the right.

I can now make the chart bigger, which is easier for you to knit from without enlarging it.

The section inside the red border of the chart is the pattern repeat. In each triangle I have 61 stitches. The pattern repeat is 12 stitches, and on Row 1, I have 6 stitches before the pattern repeat and 7 stitches after the pattern repeat. Don't count the first and last yarn over, as they are the increases and only exist on your needles after you've worked Row 1.

I have 61 stitches in each section for Chart A, which means I can work the 12-stitch pattern repeat four times.

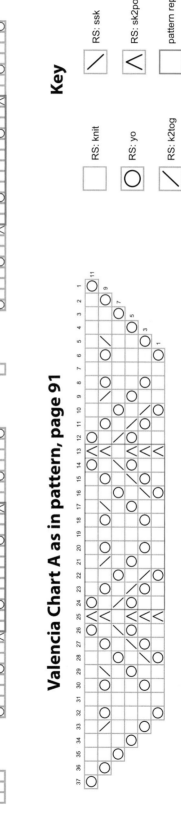

Valencia Chart A when charted fully

Valencia Chart A as in pattern, page 91

Key

/ RS: ssk	☐ RS: knit
< RS: sk2po	○ RS: yo
☐ pattern repeat	/ RS: k2tog

Row 1 (RS): Sl wyif, k2, *work row 1 of Chart A, working the 12-st rep four times*, to marked st, **k1**, *work row 1 of Chart A, working the 12-st rep four times*, to last 3 sts, k3. *4 sts inc.*

After one 12-row repeat of Chart A, you will have 153 stitches, which are broken down as follows:

- 3 stitches at the beginning of the row for the garter stitch edging
- 73 stitches for the first triangle
- 1 stitch for the center spine
- 73 stitches for the second triangle
- 3 stitches for the garter stitch edging at the end of the row

You will now work Chart A again, and this time you will work the 12-stitch repeat five times in each half of the shawl. After you've worked the 12 rows of Chart A nine times, you will have 345 stitches, which are broken down like this:

- 3 stitches at the beginning of the row for the garter stitch edging
- 169 stitches for the first triangle
- 1 stitch for the center spine
- 169 stitches for the second triangle
- 3 stitches for the garter stitch edging at the end of the row

When you start Chart B, you will have enough stitches in each half to work the 12-stitch repeat of Chart B 13 times in each half.

MADEIRA

In Madeira (page 58), you will first knit a triangle from the bottom up by increasing 1 stitch at the beginning of every row. Then, once that triangle is finished, you will pick up stitches around the triangle, and the rest of the shawl will be worked from the top down in the same way as Valencia, but you have more stitches to start with. You will increase 1 stitch after the first 2 stitches at the beginning of the row, either side of a spine stitch in the center of the row, and before the last 2 stitches at the end of the row.

Madeira illustrates the triangular shape.

Teardrop

PALMA

Palma (page 38) is a triangular shawl knitted in the same way as Valencia, except you have two increases at the beginning and end of every other row. So you will increase 6 stitches on every other row instead of 4, as you would in a triangle. So a typical row would read:

Row 5 (RS): K2, yo, k1, yo, k5, yo, **k1**, yo, k5, yo, k1, yo, k2.

As you can see, there are two yarn overs (increases) separated by a knit stitch after the first 2 stitches and before the last 2 stitches, and there is one yarn over (increase) on either side of the spine stitch (**k1**). This creates a teardrop-shaped shawl, which is a shawl with a point like a triangle, but the top edge curves quite dramatically. It's a lovely shape to wear.

Half Hexagon

NAPOLI

Napoli (page 33) is a half-hexagon-shaped shawl that is worked in the same way as Valencia. Remember in Valencia how we had two triangles separated by a spine, which created a bigger triangle? Now imagine adding another spine and another triangle. This will create a half hexagon shape like Napoli and Ibiza.

In a half-hexagon shawl, you will increase a stitch after the first 2 or 3 stitches, either side of 2 spine stitches, and before the last 2 or 3 stitches at the end of the row. So you will increase 6 stitches on every other row.

I chart a half-hexagon pattern just like I did for Valencia. So instead of charting out three identical triangles next to each other separated by two spines, I just chart one triangle. A typical row will therefore read:

Row 1 (RS): K2, (work row 1 of Chart A, **k1**) twice, work row 1 of Chart A, k2. *6 sts inc.*

The **k1** is the spine stitch. In both Palma and Napoli, you increase 6 stitches on every other row, but the resulting shape is quite different. This is because of where the increases (yarn overs) are placed in relation to one another.

A hexagon shape forms Napoli.

Hybrid Triangle

ST. TROPEZ

St. Tropez (page 110) is a cross between a half hexagon and a triangular shape, which I call a hybrid triangle. If you look at the pattern, you start by increasing 6 stitches on every other row. After a while, you stop increasing in the center section but continue increasing in the first and last section, just like you did in Valencia. This creates a really nice shape that sits better on your shoulders than a triangle shawl, but you don't end up with as many stitches as you do for a half hexagon shawl. I usually like to add a different stitch pattern to the center section to make it a special feature.

St. Tropez represents the hybrid triangle shape.

Lace Knitting Stitches

The beautiful designs in lace are created by just a few easy-to-learn stitches. You probably already know most of them, such as knit, purl, yarn over, knit 2 together, and slip, slip, knit. The lace patterns are simply created by the combination of these stitches and how they work together.

In lace patterns, every increase—typically a yarn over—is usually balanced out by a decrease. The decrease can be placed right next to the yarn over, several stitches away, or on a different row. Pattern repeats will start and end on the same stitch count, unless you are increasing. If there are more yarn overs than decreases, then you will be increasing the stitch count. If there are more decreases than yarn overs, then you will be decreasing the stitch count.

In this section, I'll walk you through the increases and decreases used in this book. Some stitches are worked slightly different for English style (also known as "throwing") and continental style (also known as "picking") knitters, and, where necessary, I have shown both styles. I am a continental knitter, so most of the technique photos are shown knitting in the continental style.

But remember the huge amount of resources available online. If you're unsure of a technique, do an online search, and you will probably find many written, photo, and video tutorials. Some tutorials are of better quality than others, so it may be worth checking a few out. Some can be found on my website, yarnaddict.co.uk.

Increases

Yarn Over (yo)

Yarn overs create the holes in lace knitting. You are increasing a stitch by taking the yarn over the right needle to create a new stitch. On the next row, this stitch is either purled or knitted.

ENGLISH-STYLE KNITTERS

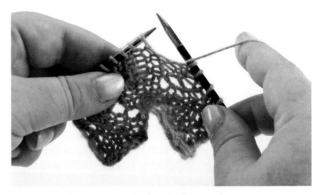

Yarn over between 2 knit stitches: Take your yarn to the front between the needles, hold it as you would if you were about to purl the next stitch, but knit the next stitch. You will now have created a loop over your right needle and increased a stitch. Please note that the yarn over is only the yarn to the front of the right needle (i.e., between the two needles to the front); the next knit stitch is a separate stitch.

Yarn over after a knit stitch and before a purl stitch: Take the yarn to the front between the needles, over the right needle to the back, and between the two needles to the front again. You will have wrapped the yarn completely around the right needle and will be ready to purl the next stitch.

Yarn over between 2 purl stitches: As you have just worked a purl stitch, the working yarn will be at the front. Take the yarn over the right needle to the back and then between the two needles to the front, ready to purl the next stitch.

Yarn over after a purl stitch and before a knit stitch: As you have just worked a purl stitch, the working yarn will be at the front. Leave the yarn at the front, then you will be ready to do a yarn over (yarn over the needle to the back) and then knit the next stitch.

CONTINENTAL-STYLE KNITTERS

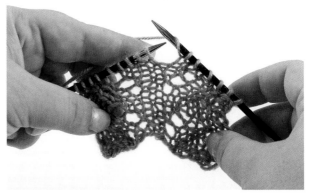

Yarn over between 2 knit stitches: Take the yarn between the needles to the front, then over the right needle to the back, ready to knit the next stitch.

If you purl with yarn at the back (Norwegian purl): Yarn overs between a knit and a purl stitch or between 2 purl stitches are worked the same way as between 2 knit stitches. You take the yarn between the needles to the front, then over the right needle to the back. You have now created the yarn over and then move your needle and yarn into the correct position to purl the next stitch.

If you purl with yarn at the front (regular continental purl): Take the yarn between the needles to the front, then over the right needle and between the needles to the front, so you are ready to purl the next stitch.

Make 1 (m1)

The make 1 increase adds one stitch without leaving a hole in the knitting as a yarn over does.

1. Lift up the strand between two stitches.

2. Place it on your left-hand needle, making sure it's sitting the same way as a regular stitch.

3. Knit through the back of this loop.

4. Finished increase.

Cable Cast-On

The cable cast-on is ueful for adding stitches during knitting.

1. Insert the right needle between the first 2 sts on the left needle.

2. Wrap yarn as if to knit and pull through a loop.

3. Transfer this st to the left needle.

4. Continue in this way, inserting the needle between the next 2 sts on the left needle, wrapping the yarn and pulling up a loop, and placing it on the left needle, until the desired number of sts are cast on.

Knit into the Front and Back and Front (kfbf)

Kfbf increases two stitches at the same time and does not leave a hole in the knitting.

1. Insert the needle into the next stitch as if to knit, wrap the yarn around the needle as if to knit and pull it through, but do not take the stitch off the left-hand needle.

2. Insert the needle into the back of the same stitch, wrap the yarn around the needle as if to knit,

and pull it through, but do not take the stitch off the left-hand needle.

3. Then insert the needle into the front of the same stitch again and wrap the yarn around as if to knit and pull it through.

4. Slip the stitch off the left-hand needle. You've now turned one stitch into three stitches.

Decreases

In lace knitting, decreases help to shape the lace pattern, so it's important to work the correct directional decreases; otherwise, it may affect the final look of your lace pattern. In garter stitch, it's less important to work directional decreases as it won't affect the final look.

Knit 2 (3) Together (k2tog/k3tog)

The k2tog decreases 1 stitch, and the k3tog decreases 2 stitches; the decrease leans to the right. Insert the right needle into 2 (3) stitches, then knit these together to make 1 stitch.

Purl 2 (3) Together (p2tog/p3tog)

As with k2tog/k3tog, this decreases 1 (2) stitches with a decrease that leans to the right when seen from the knit side of the fabric. Insert the right needle purlwise into 2 (3) stitches, then purl these together to make 1 stitch.

Slip, Slip (Slip) Knit (ssk/sssk)

This decreases 1 (2) stitches with a decrease that leans to the left. Slip the first stitch knitwise, slip the next stitch knitwise (if working a sssk, slip a third stitch knitwise), insert the tip of the left needle into the front of these 2 (3) stitches, and knit them together. You are twisting the stitches and knitting them together through the back loop.

1. Slip 1 stitch knitwise.

2. Slip the next stitch knitwise.

3. Insert the left needle into the front of both stitches and knit them together.

4. A completed ssk.

Slip, Slip (Slip) Purl (ssp/sssp)

This is the purl version of ssk/sssk and decreases 1 (2) stitches with a decrease that leans to the left when seen from the knit side. Slip 1 stitch knitwise, slip the next stitch knitwise (if working an sssp, slip a third stitch knitwise), place these stitches back on the left needle, and purl them together through the back loop.

2. Knit 2 stitches together.

The final stage (p2tog tbl) of ssp with yarn held English-style.

3. Pass the slipped stitch over.

Slip 1, Knit 2 Together, Pass Slipped Stitch Over (sk2po)

This is a double decrease and decreases from 3 stitches to 1 stitch. Slip 1 stitch knitwise, knit 2 stitches together, and pass the slipped stitch over the k2tog stitch.

1. Slip 1 stitch knitwise.

Slip 2, Knit 1, Pass 2 Slipped Stitches Over (s2kpo)

This is another double decrease and decreases from 3 stitches to 1 stitch. Slip 2 stitches (slip both together) knitwise, knit 1, and pass the 2 slipped stitches over the knit stitch.

Lace Knitting Techniques

Casting On

Long-Tail Cast-On

The long-tail cast-on can be worked over one needle, but I recommend using two needles held together. (If you use a needle size bigger than US 7/4.5 mm, use one needle in the size you'll be knitting with and one smaller size.) Casting on over two needles means you can pull each stitch tighter. When you've finished casting on, remove one needle (the smaller one, if you're using different sizes); the stitches will be perfectly even and loose enough to slide easily along your needle. Your cast-on edge will be stretchier, and those tight knots may use less yarn.

1. Measure out a tail long enough for the number of stitches you need. There are several ways of doing this, but here is my method of estimating it: Wind the yarn once around your hand; this approximates 15 to 20 stitches in lace weight yarn, 10 to 15 stitches in fingering weight yarn, 10 stitches in worsted yarn, 5 stitches in chunky. So, if I need to cast on 50 stitches in worsted-weight yarn, I wind the yarn around my hand five times.

2. Hold two needles together in your right hand. Make a slipknot and put it on the 2 needles.

3. Place the tail over your thumb and the working yarn over your index finger on your left hand.

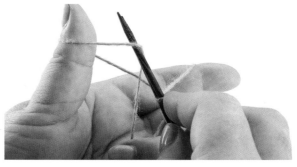

4. Grab both the tail and the working yarn with your ring finger and little finger of your left hand and hold them tight. Turn your hand so the palm of your left hand faces you.

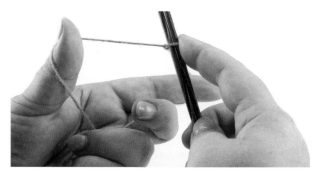

5. Move the needle toward you and under the strand that loops around your thumb.

6. Take the needle outside and under the strand that goes around your index finger.

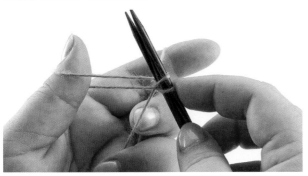

7. Take the needle through the loop that goes around your thumb, toward you.

8. Drop the loop that goes around your thumb and tighten the stitch, then pick up the tail with your thumb again. You are now ready to cast on the next stitch.

9. When you've cast on the correct number of stitches, pull one needle out, and you're ready to knit.

Binding Off

Russian Bind-Off

This gives a stretchy bind-off, which is essential for lace knitting to allow the edge to be stretched during blocking.

1. Knit 2 stitches.

2. *Insert the left needle into the front of those 2 stitches and knit both stitches together (or slip both stitches back to the left needle and knit them through the back loop).

3. This leaves 1 stitch on the right needle.

4. Knit 1.

5. Repeat from * until the correct number of stitches have been bound off. Once you've bound off the required stitches, you will be left with 1 stitch on your right needle. Break the yarn and pull it through this stitch as for a standard bind-off.

Three-Needle Bind-Off

The three-needle bind-off is a good way of joining two pieces of knitting. You won't get a completely seamless join (as with Kitchener stitch), but the seam will be smoother and less bulky than a regular seam.

Before you start, have each piece of knitting to be joined on a separate needle. Break the yarn, leaving a long tail on the piece held at the back. You will need a third needle in the pattern size. If you don't have a spare needle in the right size, then put one of the pieces to be joined on a smaller size needle so the correct size needle can be used for binding off.

The photos show the three-needle bind-off being performed by a continental knitter working a Norwegian purl (with the yarn at the back in the left hand).

Most shoulders will be joined with right sides together so the seam ends up on the wrong side of the garment. But you may at times be joining pieces knitwise. If that's the case, then knit instead of purl.

1. Hold the two pieces to be joined in your left hand with right sides together.

2. Insert the right needle into the first stitch on the back needle and the first stitch on the front needle purlwise and purl these 2 stitches together.

3. *Insert the right needle into the next stitch on the back needle and the next stitch on the front needle purlwise and purl these 2 stitches together.

4. You now have 2 stitches on the right needle.

5. Lift the first stitch over the second stitch just as in a regular bind-off. You have now bound off 1 stitch, and 1 stitch remains on the right needle.

6. Repeat from * until all stitches have been bound off.

Piece bound off with three-needle bind-off seen from the wrong side.

Piece bound off with three-needle bind-off seen from the right side.

Sewn Bind-Off

This bind-off gives a stretchier edge than a standard bind-off but not as stretchy as the Russian bind-off. I like this for binding off necklines; the top of fingerless gloves, mittens, and hand warmers; and socks.

1. Break the yarn, leaving a tail long enough to bind off all stitches (approximately three times the length to be bound off).

2. Hold the knitting needle in your left hand. Thread the yarn on a blunt tapestry needle and hold it in your right hand. Every time you take the tapestry needle into a stitch, pull the yarn all the way through.

3. *Insert the tapestry needle into the first 2 stitches purlwise, and leave both stitches on the needle.

4. Insert the tapestry needle into the first stitch *only* knitwise, and take this stitch off the knitting needle. You've now bound off 1 stitch.

5. Repeat from * until all stitches have been bound off. When you come to the last 2 stitches, complete steps 1 and 2, and then slip both stitches off the needle and fasten off the yarn.

Several stitches have been bound off with the sewn bind-off.

Finishing Techniques

When sewing up a garment or any knitting where you need to join two pieces using a seam, I recommend using the mattress stitch. It creates a seam that, although not completely invisible, blends in well with your garment.

You will be sewing with the right side facing you, which makes it easier to see how your seam is looking. I recommend practicing on two swatches using a contrasting yarn before you do it on a garment.

If you've knitted the garment in a yarn that is uneven (thick and thin), chunky, textured, or a brushed mohair, I recommend using a smooth yarn in a similar color. If you've knitted with chunky yarn then I recommend using a slightly thinner yarn for sewing to avoid bulky seams. Be careful with a single-ply yarn, a softly spun or spun woolen yarn, as it can break easily. When using single-ply, use shorter lengths of yarn as the yarn will gradually untwist as you seam and that can make it break even more easily.

If you're using a different yarn than the one your garment was knitted in, make sure the two fibers can be washed in the same way. For example, if you knitted a sweater in a superwash wool, don't use a non-superwash wool for sewing if you intend to machine wash the sweater as the non-washable wool used for sewing may felt.

1. Lay both pieces flat, side by side in front of you with right sides facing you. Use a long length of yarn and a tapestry needle. You will start between the first and second stitch from the edge. I recommend doing any increases and decreases two stitches in from the edge to give you a clear channel between the first and second stitch for seaming.

2. Insert your needle between the first and second stitch. Insert the needle under the first two horizontal strands on the right-hand piece. I normally go under two strands at a time but with thinner yarn you can go under three strands or with chunky yarn you may only want to go under one strand. It's your decision. Do not pull the yarn too tight.

3. Then insert your needle under two strands between the first and second stitch on the left-hand piece. Do not pull the yarn too tight.

4. *Back to the right-hand piece. Insert the needle into the same place you came out of last time and go under two strands of yarn.

5. In the left-hand piece, insert the needle into the same place you came out of last time and go under two strands of yarn.

1. You will be using a knitting needle and your working yarn. Pick up stitches one stitch in from the edge for the neatest result. With the right side facing, insert the needle into the fabric, wrap the yarn around your needle as to knit a stitch and pull it through to the front of the fabric.

6. Repeat from *. After about 1–2 inches (2.5–5 cm) pull on the yarn (when you're close to the start, hold on to the tail too) to "zip" up the seam. Repeat to the end of the seam.

Picking Up Stitches

This is my recommended method for picking up stitches along a piece of knitting like a button band, neckline, and collar. The pattern will say "pick up and knit."

2. To help you pick up the correct number of stitches evenly, I recommend that you evenly divide the edge where you're picking up stitches. For a button band, divide the front of your cardigan in half then divide each half in half so you have four sections. Use removable markers or short pieces of yarn. If you have four sections, divide the number of stitches you're picking up by four so you will know how many stitches to pick up in each section. A common pick-up ratio used by designers is three stitches for every four rows.

Blocking

Blocking is essential for your lace project to look its best. You will need a flat area large enough for your finished item; a towel, blanket, or blocking mat to keep the surface underneath dry; and lots of pins. Blocking wires make the job easier but are not essential.

1. Soak the piece of knitting until wet and squeeze gently in a towel.
2. Lay the piece out flat; stretch it to shape and size (measure if necessary).
3. Insert blocking wires (if using) and pin them in place. If you're not using blocking wires, pin the piece in place. Start pinning in the corners first, then add pins along the straight edges. Stretch and smooth out the lace while pinning. If you want scalloped edges or points, use one pin for each point. Don't be afraid to stretch the piece, especially if it's an accessory. With garments, check the measurements in the pattern.
4. Leave to dry completely.
5. Once dry, remove the pins. Your knitting will relax a little bit and is unlikely to stay the blocked size. Therefore, I recommend stretching it as much as possible during blocking (but if it's a garment, then do check final measurements as stated in the pattern).

Adding Beads to Your Knitting (B)

You need a crochet hook small enough for the bead to fit on it. I usually use US 13 (0.75) mm or US 15 (0.5) mm steel crochet hooks, depending on the size of the beads I'm using.

1. Place a bead on the crochet hook.

2. Lift the stitch off the left needle using the crochet hook.

3. The stitch should sit in the "hook" of the crochet hook.

4. Push the bead onto the stitch.

5. Place the stitch back on the left needle.

6. Knit the beaded stitch as normal.

Milano

Milano is worked sideways from the top corner and gradually increases in size to the lace edging, creating an asymmetrical peaked crescent, which is really easy to wear. Perfect wrapped around your neck as a scarf, it looks fantastic knitted in a gradient or self-striping yarn.

SKILL LEVEL

Level 1

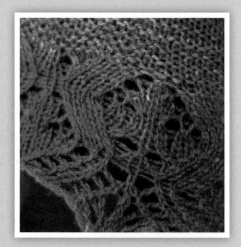

NOTES

- See page 17 for a photo tutorial on how to work the Russian bind-off.
- Charts show RS rows only; see pattern for WS rows.

Finished Measurements

Wingspan: 54 in/137 cm
Depth (along bind-off edge): 57 in/145 cm

Yarn

Freia Fine Handpaints Ombré Lace, lace weight #0 yarn, 75% wool/25% nylon, 645 yd/590 m, 2.6 oz/75 g
- 1 skein Grapevine

Needles and Other Materials

- US size 4 (3.5 mm) needles
- Tapestry needle
- Stitch markers

Gauge

20 sts x 22 rows in Chart A patt after blocking = 4 in/10 cm square
Be sure to check your gauge!

Special Stitches and Techniques

Kfbf: Knit into the front, back, and front of the same stitch; 2 stitches increased.

Sk2po: Slip 1 stitch knitwise, knit 2 stitches together, pass the slipped stitch over the k2tog stitch.

Russian bind-off: Knit 2 stitches. *Insert the left needle into the front of those 2 stitches and knit both stitches together (or slip both stitches back to the left needle and knit through the back loop). This leaves 1 stitch on the right needle. Knit 1. Repeat from * until the correct number of stitches have been bound off. Once you've bound off the required stitches, you will be left with 1 stitch on your right needle. Break the yarn and pull it through this stitch as for a normal bind-off.

Cast On

CO 8 sts. Knit 1 row.

Begin Garter Stitch

Row 1 (RS): Sl wyif, kfbf, k1, k2tog, yo, ssk, k1. *1 st inc.; 9 sts.*

Row 2 (WS and all following WS rows): Sl wyif, k to end.

Row 3: Sl wyif, kfbf, k4, yo, ssk, k1. *2 sts inc.; 11 sts.*

Row 5: Sl wyif, kfbf, k4, k2tog, yo, ssk, k1. *1 st inc.; 12 sts.*

Row 6: Sl wyif, k to end. *Rows 1–6: 4 sts inc.; 12 sts.*

Garter Stitch Repeat

Row 1 (RS): Sl wyif, kfbf, k to last 5 sts, k2tog, yo, ssk, k1. *1 st inc.*

Row 2 (WS and all following WS rows): Sl wyif, k to end.

Row 3: Sl wyif, kfbf, k to last 3 sts, yo, ssk, k1. *2 sts inc.*

Row 5: Sl wyif, kfbf, k to last 5 sts, k2tog, yo, ssk, k1. *1 st inc.*

Row 6: Sl wyif, k to end.

Rep the last 6 rows a total of 14 times. *68 sts.*

Work Chart A

Row 1 (RS): Work Row 1 of Chart A, working the 18-st rep three times. *1 st inc.*

Row 2 (WS and all following WS rows): Sl wyif, k1, p to last 2 sts, k2.

Row 3: Work Row 3 of Chart A, working the 18-st rep three times. *2 sts inc.*

Row 5: Work Row 5 of Chart A, working the 18-st rep three times. *1 st inc.*

Continue working through all 18 rows of Chart A once. *80 sts.*

Garter Stitch

Work Rows 1–6 of the Garter Stitch rep a total of six times. *104 sts.*

Work Chart A

Row 1 (RS): Work Row 1 of Chart A, working the 18-st rep five times. *1 st inc.*

Row 2 (WS and all following WS rows): Sl wyif, k1, p to last 2 sts, k2.

Row 3: Work Row 3 of Chart A, working the 18-st rep five times. *2 sts inc.*

Row 5: Work Row 5 of Chart A, working the 18-st rep five times. *1 st inc.*

Continue working through all 18 rows of Chart A once. *116 sts.*

Garter Stitch

Work Rows 1–6 of the Garter Stitch rep a total of six times. *176 sts.*

Work Chart A

Row 1 (RS): Work Row 1 of Chart A, working the 18-st rep nine times. *1 st inc.*
Row 2 (WS and all following WS rows): Sl wyif, k1, p to last 2 sts, k2.
Row 3: Work Row 3 of Chart A, working the 18-st rep nine times. *2 sts inc.*
Row 5: Work Row 5 of Chart A, working the 18-st rep nine times. *1 st inc.*
Continue working through all 18 rows of Chart A once. *188 sts.*

Work Chart B

Row 1 (RS): Work Row 1 of Chart B, working the 18-st rep 10 times. *1 st inc.*
Row 2 (WS and all following WS rows): Sl wyif, k1, p to last 2 sts, k2.
Row 3: Work Row 3 of Chart B, working the 18-st rep 10 times. *2 sts inc.*
Row 5: Work Row 5 of Chart B, working the 18-st rep 10 times. *1 st inc.*
Continue working through all 10 rows of Chart B. *195 sts.* Bind off using the Russian bind-off.

Garter Stitch

Work Rows 1–6 of the Garter Stitch rep a total of six times. *140 sts.*

Finishing

Weave in all loose ends. Soak the shawl in lukewarm water. Squeeze out excess water. Stretch the shawl to size and shape and pin in place. Leave to dry. Unpin when dry.

Work Chart A

Row 1 (RS): Work Row 1 of Chart A, working the 18-st rep seven times. *1 st inc.*
Row 2 (WS and all following WS rows): Sl wyif, k1, p to last 2 sts, k2.
Row 3: Work Row 3 of Chart A, working the 18-st rep seven times. *2 sts inc.*
Row 5: Work Row 5 of Chart A, working the 18-st rep seven times. *1 st inc.*
Continue working through all 18 rows of Chart A once. *152 sts.*

Chart A

Pattern repeats are indicated by [ ].
Row 1 (RS): Sl wyif, kfbf, [k3, k2tog, k3, yo, k1, yo, k3, ssk, k4] to last 12 sts, k3, k2tog, k2, yo, k2tog, yo, ssk, k1.
Row 2 (WS and all following WS rows): Sl wyif, k1, p to last 2 sts, k2.
Row 3: Sl wyif, kfbf, k2, [yo, ssk, k2tog, (k3, yo) twice, k3, ssk, k3] to last 11 sts, k2, k2tog, k3, yo, k1, yo, ssk, k1.

Row 5: Sl wyif, kfbf, k4, [k1, k2tog, k3, yo, k5, yo, k3, ssk, k2] to last 11 sts, k1, k2tog, k3, yo, k2tog, yo, ssk, k1.

Row 7: Sl wyif, kfbf, k6, [k2tog, k3, yo, k1, yo, ssk, k1, k2tog, yo, k1, yo, k3, ssk, k1] to last 10 sts, k2tog, k3, yo, k2tog, yo, ssk, k1.

Row 9: Sl wyif, kfbf, k to last 3 sts, yo, ssk, k1.

Row 11: Sl wyif, kfbf, k4, k2tog, k3, yo, k1, [yo, k3, ssk, k7, k2tog, k3, yo, k1] to last 9 sts, yo, ssk, k2, k2tog, yo, ssk, k1.

Row 13: Sl wyif, kfbf, k5, k2tog, k3, yo, k2, [k1, yo, k3, ssk, k2tog, yo, k1, yo, ssk, k2tog, k3, yo, k2] to last 8 sts, k1, yo, ssk, k2tog, yo, ssk, k1.

Row 15: Sl wyif, kfbf, k6, k2tog, k3, yo, k3, [k2, yo, k3, ssk, k3, k2tog, k3, yo, k3] to last 7 sts, k2, (yo, ssk) twice, k1.

Row 17: Sl wyif, kfbf, k7, k2tog, k3, yo, k1, yo, ssk, k1, [k2tog, yo, k1, yo, k3, ssk, k1, k2tog, k3, yo, k1, yo, ssk, k1] to last 7 sts, (k2tog, yo) twice, ssk, k1.

Row 18: Sl wyif, k1, p to last 2 sts, k2.

Chart B

Pattern repeats are indicated by [ ].

Row 1 (RS): Sl wyif, kfbf, [k3, k2tog, yo, k2tog, (k1, yo) twice, k1, ssk, yo, ssk, k4] to last 6 sts, k1, k2tog, yo, ssk, k1.

Row 2 (WS and all following WS rows): Sl wyif, k1, p to last 2 sts, k2.

Row 3: Sl wyif, kfbf, k2, [2, k2tog, yo, k2tog, k1, yo, k3, yo, k1, ssk, yo, ssk, k3] to last 5 sts, k2, yo, ssk, k1.

Row 5: Sl wyif, kfbf, k4, [k1, k2tog, yo, k2tog, k1, yo, k2tog, yo, k1, yo, ssk, yo, k1, ssk, yo, ssk, k2] to last 5 sts, k2tog, yo, ssk, k1.

Row 7: Sl wyif, kfbf, yo, k1, ssk, yo, ssk, k1, [k2tog, yo, k2tog, k1, yo, k2tog, yo, k3, yo, ssk, yo, k1, ssk, yo, ssk, k1] to last 4 sts, k1, yo, ssk, k1.

Row 9: Sl wyif, kfbf, k3, yo, k1, ssk, yo, sk2po, [yo, k2tog, k1, (yo, k2tog) twice, yo, k1, (yo, ssk) twice, yo, k1, ssk, yo, sk2po] to last 3 sts, yo, ssk, k1.

Row 10: Sl wyif, k1, p to last 2 sts, k2.

Key

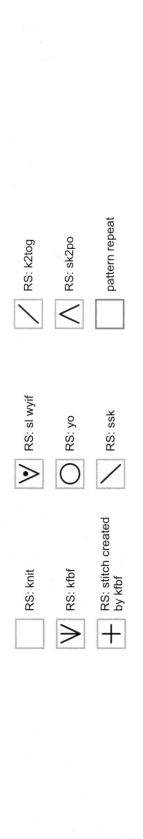

RS: knit

RS: kfbf

RS: stitch created by kfbf

RS: sl wyif

RS: yo

RS: ssk

RS: k2tog

RS: sk2po

pattern repeat

Chart A

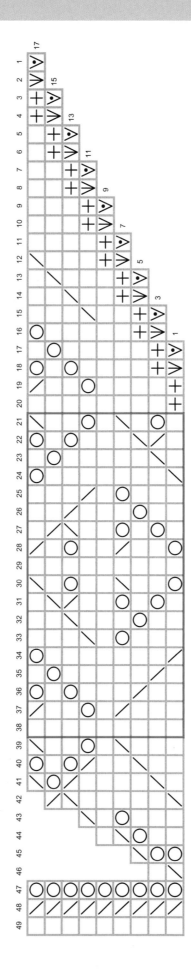

Chart B

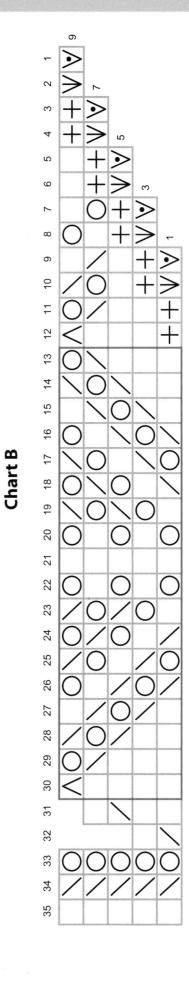

Benidorm

Benidorm is a large, simple shawl that is perfect to wrap up in. You can customize this shawl by working part 1 until you've used up half your available yarn, then work part 2.

SKILL LEVEL

Level 1

NOTES

- This shawl is worked sideways with increases inside the lace border. Once half the yarn has been used, start decreases to complete the shawl.
- See page 17 for a photo tutorial on how to work the Russian bind-off.

Finished Measurements

Wingspan: 73 in/185.5 cm
Depth: 31 in/79 cm

Yarn

Schoppel Zauberball 100, super fine weight #1 yarn, 100% superwash merino wool, 437 yd/400 m, 3.5 oz/100 g
- 2 skeins #2264 Licht im Schacht (Light in the Tunnel)

Needles and Other Materials

- US size 6 (4 mm) straight needles
- Tapestry needle
- Stitch marker

Gauge

21 sts x 22 rows in Chart A patt after blocking = 4 in/10 cm square
Be sure to check your gauge!

Special Stitches and Techniques

Sk2po: Slip 1 stitch knitwise, knit 2 stitches together, pass the slipped stitch over the k2tog stitch.

Russian bind-off: Knit 2 stitches. *Insert the left needle into the front of those 2 stitches and knit both stitches together (or slip both stitches back to the left needle and knit through back loop). This leaves 1 stitch on the right needle. Knit 1. Repeat from * until the correct number of stitches have been bound off. Once you've bound off the required stitches, you will be left with 1 stitch on your right needle. Break the yarn and pull it through this stitch as for a normal bind-off.

Cast On

CO 31 sts. Knit 1 row.

Part 1

Row 1 (RS): K2, m1, pm, work Row 1 of Chart, working the 12-st rep twice. *1 st inc.*

Row 2 (WS): Work Row 2 of Chart, working the 12-st rep twice, sm, k3.

Row 3: K3, m1, sm, work Row 3 of Chart, working the 12-st rep twice. *1 st inc.*

Row 4: Work Row 4 of Chart, working the 12-st rep twice, sm, k to end.

Row 5: K to m, m1, sm, work Row 5 of Chart, working the 12-st rep twice. *1 st inc.*

Row 6: Work Row 6 of Chart, working the 12-st rep twice, sm, k to end.

Continue as established, working through all 18 rows of Chart 14 times. *157 sts.*

Part 2

Row 1 (RS): K to 2 sts before m, k2tog, sm, work Row 1 of Chart, working the 12-st rep twice. *1 st dec.*

Row 2 (WS): Work Row 2 of Chart, working the 12-st rep twice, sm, k to end.

Row 3: K to 2 sts before m, k2tog, sm, work Row 3 of Chart, working the 12-st rep twice. *1 st dec.*

Row 4: Work Row 4 of Chart, working the 12-st rep twice, sm, k to end.

Continue working through all 18 rows of Chart 14 times. *31 sts.*

Bind off using the Russian bind-off method.

Finishing

Weave in all loose ends. Soak the shawl in lukewarm water. Squeeze out excess water. Stretch shawl to size and shape and pin in place. Leave to dry. Unpin when dry.

Chart

Pattern repeat is indicated by [ ].

Row 1 (RS): [K1, yo, ssk, k3, k2tog, k3, yo, k1] twice, k2tog, yo, k3.

Row 2 (WS and all following WS rows): K2, k2tog, yo, k1, p24.

Row 3: [K2, yo, ssk, k1, k2tog, k3, yo, k2] twice, k2tog, yo, k3.

Row 5: [K3, yo, sk2po, k3, yo, k3] twice, k2tog, yo, k3.

Row 7: [K3, k2tog, k3, yo, k4] twice, k2tog, yo, k3.

Row 9: [K2, k2tog, k3, yo, k5] twice, k2tog, yo, k3.

Row 11: [K1, k2tog, k3, yo, k1, yo, k3, k2tog] twice, k2tog, yo, k3.

Row 13: [K1, ssk, k2, yo, k3, yo, k2, k2tog] twice, k2tog, yo, k3.

Row 15: [K1, ssk, k1, yo, k5, yo, k1, k2tog] twice, k2tog, yo, k3.

Row 17: [K1, ssk, yo, k7, yo, k2tog] twice, k2tog, yo, k3.

Row 18: K2, k2tog, yo, k1, p24.

Chart

Key

□	RS: knit WS: purl
◯	RS/WS: yo
╱	RS/WS: k2tog
╲	RS: ssk
⋀	RS: sk2po
•	WS: knit
□	pattern repeat

Napoli

Napoli has a very simple lace pattern so you can focus on learning how to achieve the half-hexagon shape. Two yarns are worked in stripes from the top down. Increases every other row create the shape of this shawl, which ends with a chevron edging.

SKILL LEVEL

Level 1

NOTES

- You may wish to put a locking stitch marker on the stitches in bold, which indicate the "spines." You will increase either side of both spines on every RS row. Placing locking stitch markers on the spine stitches will help you remember to increase as directed and keep your place in the pattern.
- See page 17 for a photo tutorial on how to work the Russian bind-off.

Finished Measurements

Wingspan: 60 in/152.5 cm
Depth: 22½ in/57 cm

Yarn

Lorna's Laces Solemate, super fine weight #1 yarn, 55% superwash merino wool/15% nylon/30% Outlast, 425 yd/389 m, 3.5 oz/100 g
- 1 skein #56ns Fjord (C1)
- 1 skein #4ns Blackberry (C2)

Needles and Other Materials

- US size 6 (4 mm) circular needle, 32 in/80 cm long
- Tapestry needle
- 2 locking stitch markers

Gauge

18 sts x 32 rows in Chart patt after blocking = 4 in/10 cm square
Be sure to check your gauge!

Special Stitches and Techniques

S2kpo: Slip 2 stitches (slip both together) knitwise, knit 1, pass the 2 slipped stitches over the knit stitch.

Russian bind-off: Knit 2 stitches. *Insert the left needle into the front of those 2 stitches and knit both stitches together (or slip both stitches back to the left needle and knit through back loop). This leaves 1 stitch on the right needle. Knit 1. Repeat from * until the correct number of stitches have been bound off. Once you've bound off the required stitches, you will be left with 1 stitch on your right needle. Break the yarn and pull it through this stitch as for a normal bind-off.

Cast On

Using C2, CO 9 sts. Knit 1 row.

Garter Stitch Section

Row 1 (RS): With C1, k2, (yo, k1) five times, yo, k2. *6 sts inc.; 15 sts.*

Row 2 (WS and all following WS rows): K to end.

Row 3: With C2, k2, (yo, k3, yo, **k1**) twice, yo, k3, yo, k2. *6 sts inc.; 21 sts.*

Row 5: With C1, k2, (yo, k5, yo, **k1**) twice, yo, k5, yo, k2. *6 sts inc.; 27 sts.*

Row 7: With C2, k2, (yo, k to marked st, yo, **k1**) yo, k to last 2 sts, yo, k2. *6 sts inc.*

Continue working as established, increasing 6 sts and changing color every RS row for a total of 120 rows. *369 sts.*

Work Chart

Row 1 (RS): With C1, k2, (work Row 1 of Chart, working the 10-st rep 12 times, **k1**) twice, work Row 1 of Chart, working the 10-st rep 12 times, k2. *6 sts inc.*

Row 2 (WS): K2, (work Row 2 of Chart, working the 10-st rep 12 times, **k1**) twice, work Row 2 of Chart, working the 10-st rep 12 times, k2.

Row 3: With C2, k2, (work Row 3 of Chart, working the 10-st rep 12 times, **k1**) twice, work Row 3 of Chart, working the 10-st rep 12 times, k2.

Continue working through all 32 rows of Chart A once, changing color every RS row. *Note that the number of times to work the repeat changes on Row 21 to 13 times, and changes again on Row 23 to 14 times. Refer to the written chart instructions. 465 sts.*

Using C2, bind off using the Russian bind-off method.

Finishing

Weave in all loose ends. Soak the shawl in lukewarm water. Squeeze out excess water. Stretch the shawl to size and shape and pin in place. Leave to dry. Unpin when dry.

Pattern repeat is in [ ].
Row 1 (RS): Yo, [sl wyib, m1, k3, s2kpo, k3, m1] 12 times, sl wyib, yo.
Row 2 (WS): P1, sl wyif, [p9, sl wyif] 12 times, p1.
Row 3: Yo, k1, [k1, m1, k3, s2kpo, k3, m1] 12 times, k2, yo.
Row 4: P to end.
Row 5: Yo, k2, [sl wyib, m1, k3, s2kpo, k3, m1] 12 times, sl wyib, k2, yo.
Row 6: P3, sl wyif, [p9, sl wyif] 12 times, p3.
Row 7: Yo, k3, [k1, m1, k3, s2kpo, k3, m1] 12 times, k4, yo.
Row 8: P to end.
Row 9: Yo, k4, [sl wyib, m1, k3, s2kpo, k3, m1] 12 times, sl wyib, k4, yo.
Row 10: P5, sl wyif, [p9, sl wyif] 12 times, p5.
Row 11: Yo, k2tog, k3, m1, [k1, m1, k3, s2kpo, k3, m1] 12 times, k1, m1, k3, ssk, yo.
Row 12: K6, p1, [k9, p1] 12 times, k6.
Row 13: Yo, k1, k2tog, k3, m1, [sl wyib, m1, k3, s2kpo, k3, m1] 12 times, sl wyib, m1, k3, ssk, k1, yo.

Row 14: K7, sl wyif, [k9, sl wyif] 12 times, k7.
Row 15: Yo, k2, k2tog, k3, m1, [k1, m1, k3, s2kpo, k3, m1] 12 times, k1, m1, k3, ssk, k2, yo.
Row 16: K8, p1, [k9, p1] 12 times, k8.
Row 17: Yo, k3, k2tog, k3, m1, [sl wyib, m1, k3, s2kpo, k3, m1] 12 times, sl wyib, m1, k3, ssk, k3, yo.
Row 18: K9, sl wyif, [k9, sl wyif] 12 times, k9.
Row 19: Yo, k4, k2tog, k3, m1, [k1, m1, k3, s2kpo, k3, m1] 12 times, k1, m1, k3, ssk, k4, yo.
Row 20: K10, p1, [k9, p1] 12 times, k10.
Row 21: Yo, k1, m1, k3, s2kpo, k3, m1, [sl wyib, m1, k3, s2kpo, k3, m1] 13 times, k1, yo.
Row 22: P2, [p9, sl wyif] 13 times, p11.
Row 23: Yo, k1, [k1, m1, k3, s2kpo, k3, m1] 14 times, k2, yo.
Row 24: P to end.
Row 25: Yo, k2, [sl wyib, m1, k3, s2kpo, k3, m1] 14 times, sl wyib, k2, yo.
Row 26: P3, sl wyif, [p9, sl wyif] 14 times, p3.
Row 27: Yo, k3, [k1, m1, k3, s2kpo, k3, m1] 14 times, k4, yo.
Row 28: P to end.
Row 29: Yo, k4, [sl wyib, m1, k3, s2kpo, k3, m1] 14 times, sl wyib, k4, yo.
Row 30: K5, sl wyif, [k9, sl wyif] 14 times, k5.
Row 31: Yo, k5, [k1, m1, k3, s2kpo, k3, m1] 14 times, k6, yo.
Row 32: K to end.

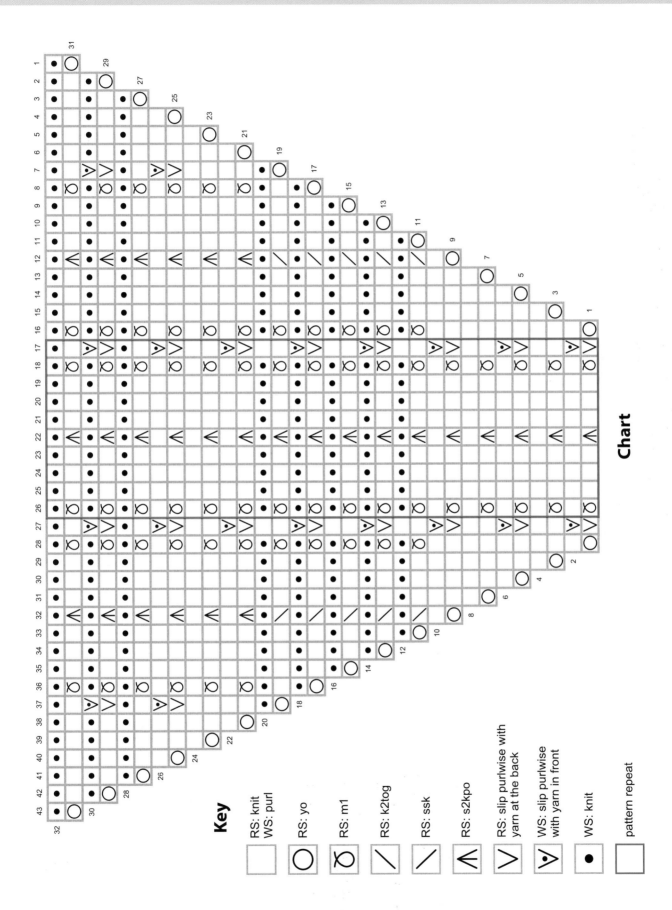

Key

☐	RS: knit / WS: purl
○	RS: yo
⊘	RS: m1
╱	RS: k2tog
╱	RS: ssk
≪	RS: s2kpo
⟩	RS: slip purlwise with yarn at the back
⟩•	WS: slip purlwise with yarn in front
•	WS: knit
☐	pattern repeat

Chart

Palma

Palma has an interesting teardrop shape that wraps around the neck nicely—perfect to wear as a scarf. The stitch pattern is easy, allowing you to focus on the shape of this shawl.

Finished Measurements

Wingspan: 50¼ in/128 cm
Depth: 22 in/56 cm

Yarn

Malabrigo Yarns Sock, super fine weight #1 yarn, 100% superwash merino wool, 440 yd/402 m, 3.5 oz/100 g
- 1 skein #SW870 Candombe

Needles and Other Materials

- US size 6 (4 mm) circular needle, 32 in/80 cm long
- Tapestry needle
- Locking stitch marker

Gauge

19 sts x 22 rows in garter st after blocking = 4 in/10 cm square
Be sure to check your gauge!

Special Stitches and Techniques

Cable cast-on (CCO): Insert the right needle between the first 2 sts on the left needle; wrap yarn as if to knit and pull through a loop. Transfer this stitch to the left needle—3 sts on the left. Insert the right needle between the first two sts as before and make a knit st on the right needle that you transfer to the left. Continue until you have the desired number of sts.

Russian bind-off (RBO): Knit 2 stitches. *Insert the left needle into the front of those 2 stitches and knit both stitches together (or slip both stitches back to the left needle and knit through the back loop). This leaves 1 stitch on the right needle. Knit 1. Repeat from * until the correct number of stitches have been bound off. Once you've bound off the required stitches, you will be left with 1 stitch on your right needle. Break the yarn and pull it through this stitch as for a normal bind-off.

SKILL LEVEL

Level 1

NOTES

- I recommend using a locking stitch marker to mark the stitch in bold, which is the spine stitch. Move the locking stitch marker up every few rows.
- Charts show RS rows only; see pattern for WS rows.
- See page 12 for a photo tutorial on how to work the cable cast-on and page 17 for the Russian bind-off.

Cast On

CO 9 sts. Knit 1 row.

Begin Shawl

Row 1 (RS): K1, (k1, yo) to last 2 sts, yo, k2. *6 sts inc.*
Row 2 (WS and all following WS rows): K to end.
Row 3: K1, (k1, yo) twice, k4, yo, **k1**, yo, k4, (yo, k1) twice, k1. *6 sts inc.*
Place a locking st marker on the stitch in bold.
Row 5: K1, (k1, yo) twice, k to center stitch, yo, **k1**, yo, k to last 3 sts, (yo, k1) twice, k1. *6 sts inc.*
Continue increasing as established on every RS row, working a total of 70 rows. *219 sts.*

Work Charts A and B

Row 1 (RS): Work Row 1 of Chart A, working the 6-st rep 17 times, **k1**, work Row 1 of Chart B, working the 6-st rep 17 times. *6 sts inc.*
Row 2 (WS and all following WS rows): K2, p to last 2 sts, k2.
Row 3: Work Row 3 of Chart A, working the 6-st rep 17 times, **k1**, work Row 3 of Chart B, working the 6-st rep 17 times. *6 sts inc.*
Continue working through all 16 rows of Charts A and B as established once. *267 sts.*

Garter Stitch Section

Row 1 (RS): K1, (k1, yo) twice, k to center stitch, yo, **k1**, yo, k to last 3 sts, (yo, k1) twice, k1. *6 sts inc.*
Row 2 (WS and all following WS rows): K to end.
Row 3: K1, (k1, yo) twice, k to center stitch, yo, **k1**, yo, k to last 3 sts, (yo, k1) twice, k1. *6 sts inc.*
Continue increasing as established on every RS row, working a total of 26 rows. *345 sts.*

Picot Bind-Off

Row 1 (RS): RBO3, [CCO2, RBO7] to last 2 sts (at this point you will have 1 st on right needle), RBO2.

Picot Bind-Off

I recommend using the cable cast-on to cast on the stitches for the picot bind-off and then use the Russian bind-off to bind off stitches. This will create a nice stretchy edge.

1. Bind off 3 stitches, then move the stitch that is on your right-hand needle back to your left-hand needle.

2. Insert the right-hand needle between the first and second stitch on your left-hand needle.

3. Knit up a new stitch.

4. Do not slip the stitch off your left-hand needle and place the new stitch on the left-hand needle.

5. *Insert the right-hand needle between the new first and second stitch on the left-hand needle.

6. Knit up a new stitch and place this stitch on the left-hand needle (do not slip the original stitch off).
7. Repeat from * until you've cast on the required number of stitches (usually two or three).

8. You will now bind off using the Russian bind-off. Knit two stitches.

9. Insert the left needle into the front of those two stitches from the left and knit them together.
10. Bind off the required number of stitches, then start casting on using the cable cast-on again.

Finishing

Weave in all loose ends. Soak the shawl in lukewarm
water. Squeeze out excess water. Stretch the shawl
to size and shape and pin in place. Leave to dry.
Unpin when dry.

Below are the written instructions for both Charts A
and B, including the **k1** center spine stitch.

Pattern repeat is in [ ]. The first time you work through
Charts A and B, work the 6 st rep 17 times in each
half. The second time you work through Charts A
and B, work the 6 st rep 29 times in each half. This
will change the number of repeats specified on rows
5, 11, and 13.

Row 1 (RS): K2, (yo, k1) twice, k2tog, yo, [k1, yo, ssk, k1,
k2tog, yo] 17 (29) times, k1, yo, **k1**, yo, [k1, yo, ssk, k1,
k2tog, yo] 17 (29) times, k1, yo, ssk, (k1, yo) twice, k2.

Row 2 (WS and all following WS rows): K2, p to last 2
sts, k2.

Row 3: K2, yo, k1, yo, k3, k2tog, yo, [k1, yo, ssk, k1,
k2tog, yo] 17 (29) times, k2, yo, **k1**, yo, k1, [k1, yo, ssk,
k1, k2tog, yo] 17 (29) times, k1, yo, ssk, k3, yo, k1, yo,
k2.

Row 5: K2, yo, k1, yo, k1, [k1, k2tog, yo, k1, yo, ssk] 18
(30) times, k3, yo, **k1**, yo, k2, [k1, k2tog, yo, k1, yo, ssk]
18 (30) times, k2, yo, k1, yo, k2.

Row 7: K2, (yo, k1) twice, yo, ssk, [k1, k2tog, yo, k1, yo,
ssk] 18 (30) times, k1, k2tog, yo, k1, yo, **k1**, yo, k1, yo,
ssk, [k1, k2tog, yo, k1, yo, ssk] 18 (30) times, k1, k2tog,
(yo, k1) twice, yo, k2.

Row 9: K2, yo, k1, yo, k3, k2tog, yo, [k1, yo, ssk, k1,
k2tog, yo] 18 (30) times, k1, yo, ssk, k2, yo, **k1**, yo, k2,
k2tog, yo, [k1, yo, ssk, k1, k2tog, yo] 18 (30) times, k1,
yo, ssk, k3, yo, k1, yo, k2.

Row 11: K2, [yo, k1] twice, [k1, yo, ssk, k1, k2tog, yo] 19
(31) times, k1, yo, ssk, k3, yo, **k1**, yo, k3, k2tog, yo, [k1,
yo, ssk, k1, k2tog, yo] 19 (31) times, k2, yo, k1, yo, k2.

Row 13: K2, (yo, k1) twice, yo, ssk, [k1, k2tog, yo, k1, yo,
ssk] 20 (32) times, k1, yo, **k1**, yo, [k1, k2tog, yo, k1, yo,
ssk] 20 (32) times, k1, k2tog, (yo, k1) twice, yo, k2.

Row 15: K2, yo, k1, yo, k3, yo, ssk, [k1, k2tog, yo, k1, yo,
ssk] 20 (32) times, k2, yo, **k1**, yo, k1, [k1, k2tog, yo, k1,
yo, ssk] 20 (32) times, k1, k2tog, yo, k3, yo, k1, yo, k2.

Row 16: K2, p to last 2 sts, k2.

Chart A

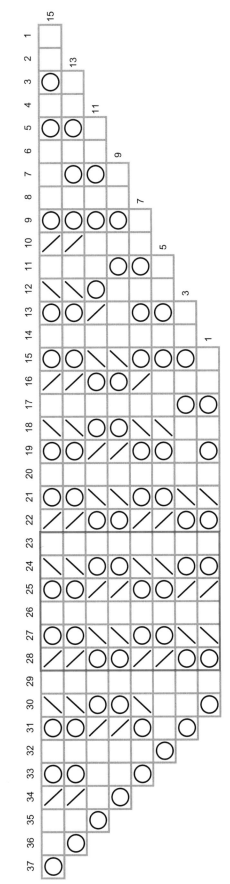

Chart B

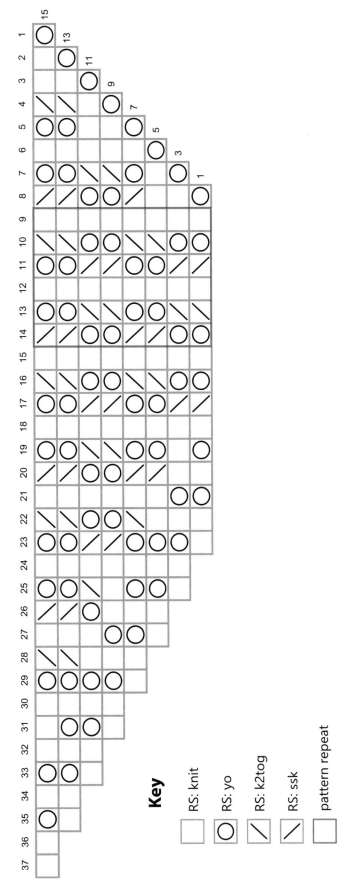

Key

☐	RS: knit
◯	RS: yo
╲	RS: k2tog
╱	RS: ssk
☐	pattern repeat

Malaga

This scarf has an interesting stitch pattern that looks good on both right and wrong sides. It is also easy to customize: Make it longer or shorter, wider or narrower. If you like, sew the ends together to make it an infinity scarf, which can be worn either as one long loop around the neck or looped around twice.

Finished Measurements

Width: 15 in/38 cm
Length: 74 in/188 cm

Yarn

Knit Picks Swish DK, light weight #3 yarn, 100% superwash merino wool, 123 yd/113 m, 1.75 oz/50 g
- 4 skeins #24953 Sugar Plum

Needles and Other Materials

- US size 8 (5 mm) straight needles
- Tapestry needle

Gauge

13 sts x 18 rows in Chart patt after blocking = 4 in/10 cm square
Be sure to check your gauge!

Special Stitches and Techniques

Sk2po: Slip 1 stitch knitwise, knit 2 stitches together, pass slipped stitch over the k2tog stitch.

Russian bind-off: Knit 2 stitches. *Insert the left needle into the front of those 2 stitches and knit both stitches together (or slip both stitches back to the left needle and knit through back loop). This leaves 1 stitch on the right needle. Knit 1. Repeat from * until the correct number of stitches have been bound off. Once you've bound off the required stitches, you will be left with 1 stitch on your right needle. Break the yarn and pull it through this stitch as for a normal bind-off.

SKILL LEVEL

Level 1

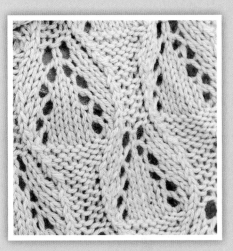

NOTES

- If you would like a wider or narrower scarf, add or subtract stitches in groups of 14.
- If you would like a longer or shorter scarf, work more or fewer 24-row chart repeats.
- To make an infinity scarf, sew the ends together.
- See page 17 for a photo tutorial on how to work the Russian bind-off.

Begin Scarf

CO 49 sts.

Row 1: Work Row 1 of Chart, working the 14-st rep three times.

Row 2: Work Row 2 of Chart, working the 14-st rep three times.

Continue working through all 24 rows of Chart a total of 14 times.

Bind off using the Russian bind-off.

Finishing

Weave in all loose ends. Soak the scarf in lukewarm water. Squeeze out excess water. Stretch the scarf to size and shape and pin in place. Leave to dry. Unpin when dry.

Chart

Pattern repeat is indicated by [ ].

Row 1 (RS): Sl wyif, k2, [k1, yo, k1, ssk, p7, k2tog, k1, yo] three times, k4.

Row 2 (WS): Sl wyif, k2, p1, [p3, k7, p4] three times, k3.

Row 3: Sl wyif, k2, [k1, yo, k2, ssk, p5, k2tog, k2, yo] three times, k4.

Row 4: Sl wyif, k2, p1, [p4, k5, p5] three times, k3.

Row 5: Sl wyif, k2, [k2, yo, k2, ssk, p3, k2tog, k2, yo, k1] three times, k4.

Row 6: Sl wyif, k2, p1, [p5, k3, p6] three times, k3.

Row 7: Sl wyif, k2, [k2, yo, k2, k2tog, p3, ssk, k2, yo, k1] three times, k4.

Row 8: Sl wyif, k2, p1, [p5, k3, p6] three times, k3.

Row 9: Sl wyif, k2, [k3, yo, k1, k2tog, p3, ssk, k1, yo, k2] three times, k4.

Row 10: Sl wyif, k2, p1, [p5, k3, p6] three times, k3.

Row 11: Sl wyif, k2, [k3, yo, k1, k2tog, p3, ssk, k1, yo, k2] three times, k4.

Row 12: Sl wyif, k2, p1, [p5, k3, p6] three times, k3.

Row 13: Sl wyif, k2, [p4, k2tog, (k1, yo) twice, k1, ssk, p3] three times, p1, k3.

Row 14: Sl wyif, k3, [k3, p7, k4] three times, k3.

Row 15: Sl wyif, k2, [p3, k2tog, k2, yo, k1, yo, k2, ssk, p2] three times, p1, k3.

Row 16: Sl wyif, k3, [k2, p9, k3] three times, k3.

Row 17: Sl wyif, k2, [p2, k2tog, k2, yo, k3, yo, k2, ssk, p1] three times, p1, k3.

Row 18: Sl wyif, k3, [k1, p11, k2] three times, k3.

Row 19: Sl wyif, k2, [p2, ssk, k2, yo, k3, yo, k2, k2tog, p1] three times, p1, k3.

Row 20: Sl wyif, k3, [k1, p11, k2] three times, k3.

Row 21: Sl wyif, k2, [p2, ssk, k1, yo, k5, yo, k1, k2tog, p1] three times, p1, k3.

Row 22: Sl wyif, k3, [k1, p11, k2] three times, k3.

Row 23: Sl wyif, k2, [p2, ssk, k1, yo, k5, yo, k1, k2tog, p1] three times, p1, k3.

Row 24: Sl wyif, k3, [k1, p11, k2] three times, k3.

Chart

Key

☐	RS: knit / WS: purl
○	RS: yo
/	RS: k2tog
\	RS: ssk
V̥	RS/WS: slip purlwise with yarn in front
•	RS: purl / WS: knit
☐	pattern repeat

Paphos

A simple stitch pattern, like the one in this design, can be used for a scarf or expanded into a cozy afghan. Either way, you will have an elegant, beautiful knitted piece to keep you warm.

Finished Measurements

Scarf
Width: 12 in/30.5 cm
Length: 68 in/173 cm
Afghan
Width: 31 in/79 cm
Length: 84 in/213 cm

Yarn

Cascade 220 Superwash, light weight #3 yarn/medium weight #4 yarn, 100% superwash wool, 220 yd/200 m, 3.5 oz/100 g
- Scarf: 3 skeins #837 Berry Pink
- Afghan: 6 skeins #867 Lichen

Needles and Other Materials

- US size 8 (5 mm) needles (a 32 in/80 cm or 40 in/100 cm circular needle is recommended for the afghan)
- Tapestry needle

Gauge

15 sts x 19 rows in Chart patt after blocking = 4 in/10 cm square
Be sure to check your gauge!

Special Stitches and Techniques

Sk2po: Slip 1 stitch knitwise, knit 2 stitches together, pass the slipped stitch over the k2tog stitch.

Russian bind-off: Knit 2 stitches. *Insert the left needle into the front of those 2 stitches and knit both stitches together (or slip both stitches back to the left needle and knit through back loop). This leaves 1 stitch on the right needle. Knit 1. Repeat from * until the correct number of stitches have been bound off. Once you've bound off the required stitches, you will be left with 1 stitch on your right needle. Break the yarn and pull it through this stitch as for a normal bind-off.

SKILL LEVEL

Level 1

NOTES

- To alter the width of the scarf or the afghan, add or subtract stitches in groups of 20.
- To make it longer or shorter, work more or fewer repeats.
- See page 17 for a photo tutorial on how to work the Russian bind-off.

Scarf

CO 46 sts. Knit 1 row.

Row 1 (RS): Work Row 1 of Chart, working the 20-st rep once.

Row 2 (WS and all following WS rows): Work Row 2 of Chart, working the 20-st rep once.

Row 3: Work Row 3 of Chart, working the 20-st rep once.

Continue working through all 18 rows of the Chart a total of 15 times, or until you reach the desired length.

Bind off using the Russian bind-off.

Afghan

CO 126 sts.

Begin Garter Stitch Border

Row 1 (RS): K to end.
Row 2 (WS): Sl wyif, k to end.
Row 3: Sl wyif, k to end.
Row 4: Sl wyif, k to end.

Commence Chart

Row 1 (RS): Work Row 1 of Chart, working the 20-st rep five times.

Row 2 (WS and all following WS rows): Work Row 2 of Chart, working the 20-st rep five times.

Row 3: Work Row 3 of Chart, working the 20-st rep five times.

Continue working through all 18 rows of the Chart a total of 22 times, or until you reach the desired length.

Garter Stitch Edge

Row 1 (RS): K to end.
Row 2 (WS): Sl wyif, k to end.
Row 3: Sl wyif, k to end.
Row 4: Sl wyif, k to end.

Bind off using the Russian bind-off.

Finishing
(both scarf and afghan)

Weave in all loose ends. Soak the piece in lukewarm water. Squeeze out excess water in a towel; be especially careful with the afghan as it'll be very heavy when full of water. Stretch the piece to size and shape and pin in place. Leave to dry. Unpin when dry.

Chart

Pattern repeat is indicated by [ ].

Row 1 (RS): Sl wyif, k6, k2tog, k3, yo, p1, [p1, k3, k2tog, k3, yo, p2, yo, k3, ssk, k3, p1] to last 13 sts, p1, yo, k3, ssk, k7.

Row 2 (WS and all following WS rows): Sl wyif, k3, p8, k1, [k1, p8, k2, p8, k1] to last 13 sts, k1, p8, k4.

Row 3: Sl wyif, k5, k2tog, k3, yo, k1, p1, [p1, k2, k2tog, k3, yo, k1, p2, k1, yo, k3, ssk, k2, p1] to last 13 sts, p1, k1, yo, k3, ssk, k6.

Row 5: Sl wyif, k4, k2tog, k3, yo, k2, p1, [p1, k1, k2tog, k3, yo, k2, p2, k2, yo, k3, ssk, k1, p1] to last 13 sts, p1, k2, yo, k3, ssk, k5.

Row 7: Sl wyif, k3, k2tog, k3, yo, k3, p1, [p1, k2tog, k3, yo, k3, p2, k3, yo, k3, ssk, p1] to last 13 sts, p1, k3, yo, k3, ssk, k4.

Row 9: Repeat Row 1.

Row 11: Repeat Row 3.

Row 13: Repeat Row 5.

Row 15: Sl wyif, k3, yo, ssk, k1, k2tog, yo, k3, p1, [p1, yo, ssk, k1, k2tog, yo, k3, p2, k3, yo, ssk, k1, k2tog, yo, p1] to last 13 sts, p1, k3, yo, ssk, k1, k2tog, yo, k4.

Row 17: Sl wyif, k4, yo, sk2po, yo, k4, p1, [p1, k1, yo, sk2po, yo, k4, p2, k4, yo, sk2po, yo, k1, p1] to last 13 sts, p1, k4, yo, sk2po, yo, k5.

Row 18: Sl wyif, k3, p8, k1, [k1, p8, k2, p8, k1] to last 13 sts, k1, p8, k4.

Chart

Key

	RS: knit WS: purl		RS: sk2po
○	RS: yo	●	RS: purl WS: knit
╱	RS: ssk	⟩	RS/WS: slip purlwise with yarn in front
╲	RS: k2tog		pattern repeat

Ayia Napa

These super-easy hand warmers are worked flat and then seamed, leaving a gap for the thumb. If you'd like a longer or shorter pair, add or work fewer pattern repeats.

SKILL LEVEL

Level 1

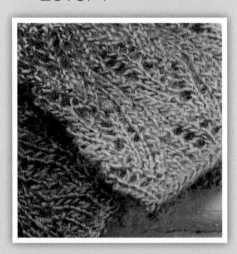

Finished Measurements

Sizes: Small (Large)
Circumference (very lightly stretched): 7 (8^1/$_2$) in/18 (21.5) cm
Length (both sizes): 10 in/25.5 cm
Hand warmers will stretch to fit a larger hand.

Yarn

Debbie Bliss Rialto Luxury Sock, super fine weight #1, 75% wool/25% polyamide, 437 yd/400 m, 3.5 oz/100 g
• 1 skein #13 Montreux

Needles and Other Materials

• US size 3 (3.25 mm) straight needles
• Tapestry needle
• Stitch markers

Gauge

28^1/$_2$ sts x 41^1/$_2$ rows in Chart A or B patt = 4 in/10 cm square
Be sure to check your gauge!

Special Stitches and Techniques

Sewn bind-off: Break the yarn, leaving a tail approximately three times the length of the bind-off edge. Using a blunt tapestry needle, *insert the tapestry needle into the first 2 sts purlwise, pull yarn all the way through, leaving the sts on the knitting needle. Insert the tapestry needle into the first st again knitwise, and slip this st off the knitting needle; rep from * to end.

Cast On

CO 50 (60) sts.

Work Rib

Size Small Only
Row 1 (RS): [P1, k4] to end.
Row 2 (WS): [P4, k1] to end.
Rep last 2 rows once more.

Size Large Only
Row 1 (RS): [P1, k4, p2, k4, p1] to end.
Row 2 (WS): [K1, p4, k2, p4, k1] to end.
Rep last 2 rows once more.

Work Chart A (B)
(both sizes)

Work Chart A for size Small and Chart B for size Large.

Row 1 (RS): Work Row 1 of Chart A (B), working the 10 (12) st rep five times.
Row 2 (WS): Work Row 2 of Chart A (B), working the 10 (12) st rep five times.
Continue working through all 16 rows of Chart A (B) six times.

Work Rib

Size Small Only
Row 1 (RS): [P1, k4] to end.
Row 2 (WS): [P4, k1] to end.
Rep last 2 rows once more.
Bind off using the sewn bind-off.

Size Large Only
Row 1 (RS): [P1, k4, p2, k4, p1] to end.
Row 2 (WS): [K1, p4, k2, p4, k1] to end.
Rep last 2 rows once more.
Bind off using the sewn bind-off.

Finishing (both sizes)

Fold each piece in half lengthwise and seam, leaving a hole for the thumb. Weave in all loose ends. Block if desired.

Chart A (size Small)

Row 1 (RS): [P1, k3, k2tog, p1, yo, k1, yo, k2tog] five times.
Row 2 (WS and all following WS rows): [P4, k1] to end.
Row 3: [P1, k2, k2tog, k1, p1, yo, k1, yo, k2tog] five times.
Row 5: [P1, k1, k2tog, k2, p1, yo, k1, yo, k2tog] five times.
Row 7: [P1, k2tog, k3, p1, yo, k1, yo, k2tog] five times.
Row 9: [P1, ssk, yo, k1, yo, p1, ssk, k3] five times.
Row 11: [P1, ssk, yo, k1, yo, p1, k1, ssk, k2] five times.
Row 13: [P1, ssk, yo, k1, yo, p1, k2, ssk, k1] five times.
Row 15: [P1, ssk, yo, k1, yo, p1, k3, ssk] five times.
Row 16: [P4, k1] to end.

Chart B (size Large)

Row 1 (RS): [P1, k3, k2tog, p2, yo, k1, yo, k2tog, p1] five times.
Row 2 (WS and all WS rows): [K1, p4, k2, p4, k1] to end.
Row 3: [P1, k2, k2tog, k1, p2, yo, k1, yo, k2tog, p1] five times.
Row 5: [P1, k1, k2tog, k2, p2, yo, k1, yo, k2tog, p1] five times.
Row 7: [P1, k2tog, k3, p2, yo, k1, yo, k2tog, p1] five times.
Row 9: [P1, ssk, yo, k1, yo, p2, ssk, k3, p1] five times.
Row 11: [P1, ssk, yo, k1, yo, p2, k1, ssk, k2, p1] five times.
Row 13: [P1, ssk, yo, k1, yo, p2, k2, ssk, k1, p1] five times.
Row 15: [P1, ssk, yo, k1, yo, p2, k3, ssk, p1] five times.
Row 16: [K1, p4, k2, p4, k1] to end.

Chart A (size Small)

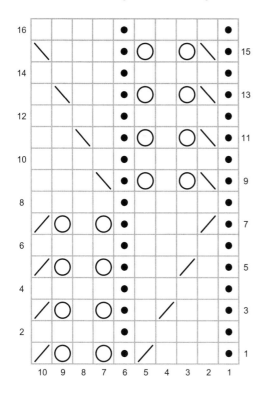

Chart B (size Large)

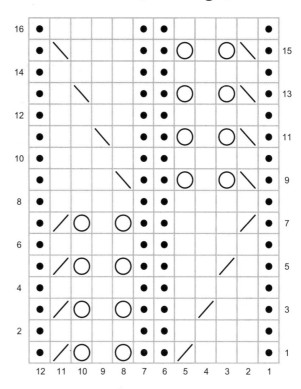

Key

	RS: knit WS: purl
●	RS: purl WS: knit
◯	RS: yo
╲	RS: ssk
╱	RS: k2tog

Madeira

Madeira is inspired by traditional Shetland hap shawls, which were everyday shawls worn by Shetland women. They were simpler than the elaborate lace shawls the Shetlands are known for. Madeira has a dramatic big eyelet border worked in a contrasting yarn.

Finished Measurements

Wingspan: 67 in/170 cm
Depth: 33 in/84 cm

Yarn

Debbie Bliss Fine Donegal, super fine weight #1 yarn, 95% wool/5% cashmere, 415 yd/380 m, 3.5 oz/100 g

- 1 skein #25 Wisteria (C1)
- 1 skein #09 Fuchsia (C2)

Needles and Other Materials

- US size 6 (4 mm) straight needles
- US size 6 (4 mm) circular needle, 40 in/100 cm long
- Tapestry needle
- Locking stitch marker

Gauge

15 sts x 31½ rows in garter st after blocking = 4 in/10 cm square
Be sure to check your gauge!

Special Stitches and Techniques

Sewn bind-off: Break the yarn, leaving a tail approximately three times the length of the bind-off edge. Using a blunt tapestry needle, *insert the tapestry needle into the first 2 sts purlwise, pull the yarn all the way through, leaving the sts on the knitting needle. Insert the tapestry needle into the first st again knitwise, and slip this st off the knitting needle; rep from * to end.

Russian bind-off: Knit 2 stitches. *Insert the left needle into the front of those 2 stitches and knit both stitches together (or slip both stitches back to the left needle and knit through back loop). This leaves 1 stitch on the right needle. Knit 1. Repeat from * until the correct number of stitches have been bound off. Once you've bound off the required stitches, you will be left with 1 stitch on your right needle. Break the yarn and pull it through this stitch as for a normal bind-off.

SKILL LEVEL

Level 2

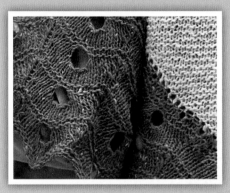

NOTES

- This shawl starts with the inner triangle. Yarn overs worked at the beginning of every row create the triangular shape. These yarn overs are later picked up, and the lace border is worked from the top down.
- See photo tutorials on how to work the Russian bind-off on page 17 and sewn bind-off on page 19.
- I recommend using a locking stitch marker to mark the stitch in bold, which is the spine stitch, to remind you to make the increases on either side. Move the locking stitch marker up every few rows.
- The stitch count of each pattern repeat increases on Rows 5 and 15 and gradually returns to normal on subsequent 4 rows.

Picking Up Stitches for the Madeira Shawl

The Madeira Shawl has yarn overs at the beginning of every row on the body, which will leave loops where you will pick up stitches for the border.

I prefer to pick up all the loops onto a long circular needle, then go back to the beginning and knit all the stitches.

1. With the right side facing, start from the top left-hand corner and pick up each loop along the edge. Make sure the loops sit on the needle as a regular stitch.

2. Continue to pick up stitches all the way around the shawl. You may wish to put a marker in the center stitch (at the bottom of the triangle, which is not shown in the photo).

3. Then go back and knit those loops.

Part 1

Using C1, CO 1. Place a locking stitch marker on this stitch.

Row 1 (RS): Yo, k1. *1 st inc.*
Row 2 (WS): Yo, k2. *1 st inc.*
Row 3: Yo, k to end. *1 st inc.*
Row 4: Yo, k to end. *1 st inc.*

Continue as established until a total of 190 rows have been worked. *191 sts. You'll have 95 loops on each side.*

Bind off using the sewn bind-off.

Part 2

Setup row: Using C2 and a long circular needle, with the RS facing, start at the top left corner, pick up and k95 sts in the yo loops along one side, pick up and **k1** in the marked cast-on st (remove the marker and place it on this new st). Pick up and k95 sts in the yo loops along the other side. *191 sts.*

Note: The stitch in bold is the center stitch, and I recommend placing a locking stitch marker in this stitch.

Row 2 (WS): K2, (yo, k3) 31 times, yo, **k1,** (yo, k3) 31 times, yo, k2. *255 sts.*

Work Chart A

Row 1 (RS): K2, work Row 1 of Chart A, working the 14-st rep eight times, **k1**, work Row 1 of Chart A, working the 14-st rep eight times, k2. *4 sts inc.*
Row 2 (WS): K2, work Row 2 of Chart A, working the 14-st rep eight times, **k1**, work Row 2 of Chart A, working the 14-st rep eight times, k2.
Row 3: K2, work Row 3 of Chart A, working the 14-st rep eight times, **k1**, work Row 3 of Chart A, working the 14-st rep eight times, k2. *4 sts inc.*

Continue working through all 20 rows of Chart A once. *295 sts.*

Work Chart B

Row 1 (RS): K2, work Row 1 of Chart B, working the 14-st rep 10 times, **k1**, work Row 1 of Chart B, working the 14-st rep 10 times, k2. *4 sts inc.*
Row 2 (WS): K2, work Row 2 of Chart B, working the 14-st rep 10 times, **k1**, work Row 2 of Chart B, working the 14-st rep 10 times, k2.

Row 3: K2, work Row 3 of Chart B, working the 14-st rep 10 times, **k1**, work Row 3 of Chart B, working the 14-st rep 10 times, k2. *4 sts inc.*
Continue working through all 20 rows of Chart B once. *335 sts.*

Edging

Row 1 (RS): K2, yo, k to center st, yo, **k1**, yo, k to last 2 sts, yo, k2. *4 sts inc.*
Row 2 (WS): K to end.
Row 3: K2, yo, k to center st, yo, **k1**, yo, k to last 2 sts, yo, k2. *4 sts inc.*
Row 4: K to end.
BO using the Russian bind-off method.

Finishing

Weave in all loose ends. Soak the shawl in lukewarm water. Squeeze out excess water. Stretch the shawl to size and shape and pin in place. Leave to dry. Unpin when dry.

Chart A

Pattern repeat is indicated by [ ].
Row 1 (RS): Yo, k125, yo.
Row 2 (WS): K to end.
Row 3: Yo, k127, yo.
Row 4: K to end.
Row 5: Yo, k8, [k2tog, k5, (yo) six times, k5, ssk] eight times, k9, yo.
Row 6: P10, [p7, (p1 tbl, p1) twice, p1 tbl, p6] eight times, p9.
Row 7: Yo, k9, [k2tog, k5, (k1 tbl, k1) twice, k1 tbl, k4, ssk] eight times, k10, yo.
Row 8: P to end.
Row 9: Yo, k10, [k2tog, k12, ssk] eight times, k11, yo.
Row 10: P to end.
Row 11: Yo, k135, yo.
Row 12: K to end.
Row 13: Yo, k137, yo.
Row 14: K to end.
Row 15: Yo, k13, [k2tog, k5, (yo) six times, k5, ssk] eight times, k14, yo.
Row 16: P15, [p7, (p1 tbl, p1) twice, p1 tbl, p6] eight times, p14.

Row 17: Yo, k14, [k2tog, k5, (k1 tbl, k1) twice, k1 tbl, k4, ssk] eight times, k15, yo.
Row 18: P to end.
Row 19: Yo, k15, [k2tog, k12, ssk] eight times, k16, yo.
Row 20: P to end.

Chart B

Pattern repeat is indicated by [ ].
Row 1 (RS): Yo, k145, yo.
Row 2 (WS): K to end.
Row 3: Yo, k147, yo.
Row 4: K to end.
Row 5: Yo, k4, [k2tog, k5, (yo) six times, k5, ssk] 10 times, k5, yo.
Row 6: P6, [p7, (p1 tbl, p1) twice, p1 tbl, p6] 10 times, p5.
Row 7: Yo, k5, [k2tog, k5, (k1 tbl, k1) twice, k1 tbl, k4, ssk] 10 times, k6, yo.

Row 8: P to end.
Row 9: Yo, k6, [k2tog, k12, ssk] 10 times, k7, yo.
Row 10: P to end.
Row 11: Yo, k155, yo.
Row 12: K to end.
Row 13: Yo, k157, yo.
Row 14: K to end.
Row 15: Yo, k9, [k2tog, k5, (yo) six times, k5, ssk] 10 times, k10, yo.

Row 16: P11, [p7, (p1 tbl, p1) twice, p1 tbl, p6] 10 times, p10.
Row 17: Yo, k10, [k2tog, k5, (k1 tbl, k1) twice, k1 tbl, k4, ssk] 10 times, k11, yo.
Row 18: P to end.
Row 19: Yo, k11, [k2tog, k12, ssk] 10 times, k12, yo.
Row 20: P to end.

Chart A

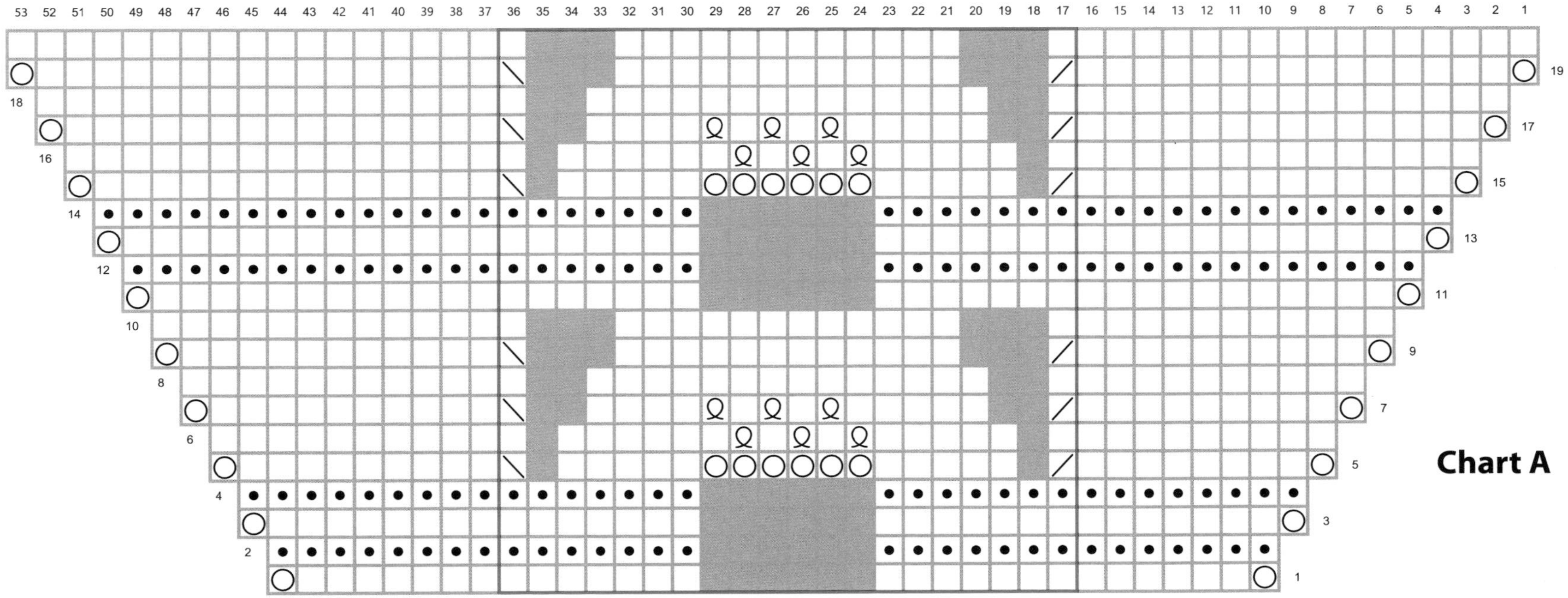

Chart B

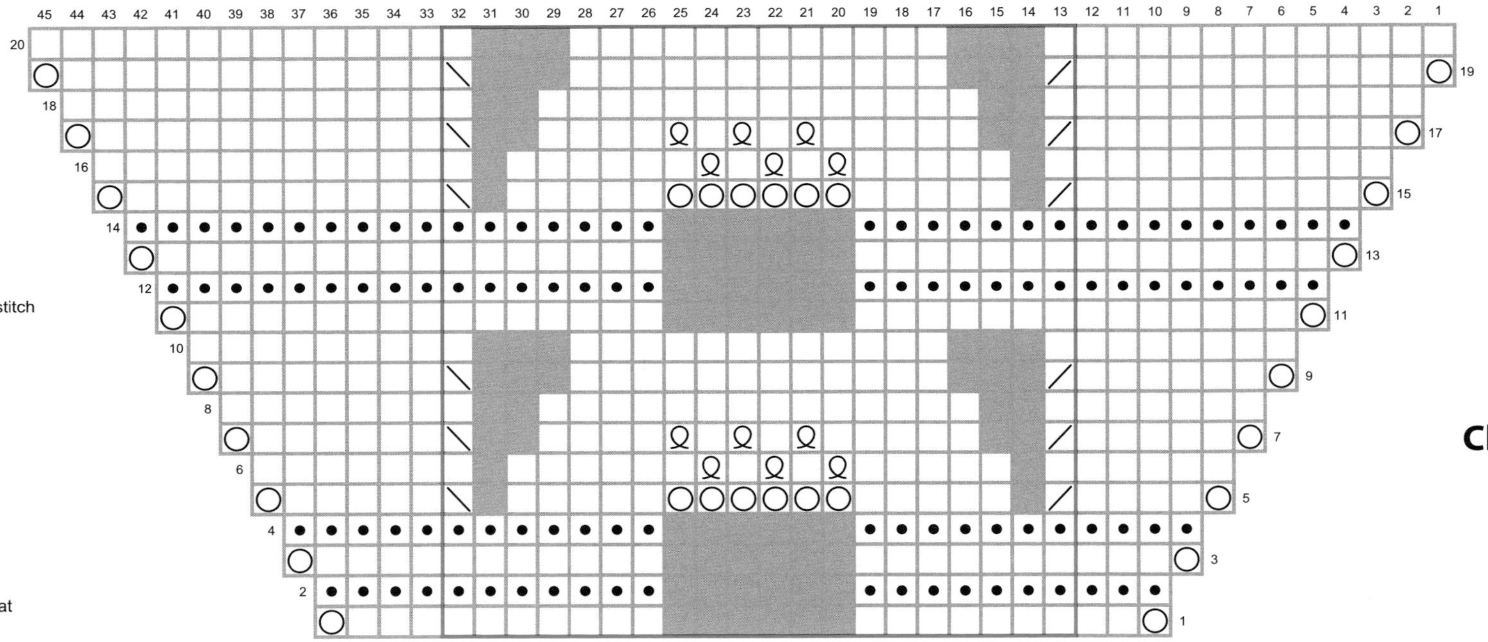

Key

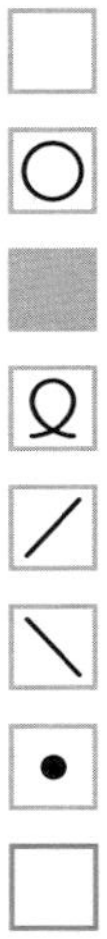

RS: knit
WS: purl

RS: yo

RS/WS: no stitch

RS: k1 tbl
WS: p1 tbl

RS: k2tog

RS: ssk

WS: knit

pattern repeat

Firenze

This simple cowl is worked in the round using two colors. It makes a nice, quick project for practicing lace knitting techniques. Just pop it on as you head out on chilly days; it goes great with everything!

Finished Measurements

Circumference: 26 in/66 cm
Depth: 12 in/30.5 cm

Yarn

Debbie Bliss Rialto 4 Ply, fine weight #2 yarn, 100% extra fine merino wool, 197 yd/180 m, 1.75 oz/50 g
- 2 balls #49 Leaf (C1)
- 2 balls #06 Stone (C2)

Needles and Other Materials

- US size 6 (4 mm) circular needle, 16 in/40 cm long
- Tapestry needle
- Stitch marker

Gauge

18½ sts x 26 rows in Chart patt after blocking = 4 in/10 cm square
Be sure to check your gauge!

Special Stitches and Techniques

Sk2po: Slip 1 stitch knitwise, knit 2 stitches together, pass the slipped stitch over the k2tog stitch.

Sewn bind-off: Break the yarn, leaving a tail approximately three times the length of the bind-off edge. Using a blunt tapestry needle, *insert the tapestry needle into the first 2 sts purlwise, pull the yarn all the way through, leaving the sts on the knitting needle. Insert tapestry needle into the first st again knitwise and slip this st off the knitting needle; rep from * to end.

NOTES

- If you would like a cowl with a larger circumference, add stitches in groups of 10.
- See page 19 for a photo tutorial on the sewn bind-off.

Continue working through all 12 rnds of Chart, changing to C2 on Rnds 9–12. Work the Chart a total of six times, always working Rnds 1–8 in C1 and Rnds 9–12 in C2.

Edging

Rnd 1: With C2, k to end.
Rnd 2: P to end.
Bind off using the sewn bind-off method.

Finishing

Weave in all loose ends. Soak the cowl in lukewarm water. Squeeze out excess water. Stretch the cowl to size and pin in place. Leave to dry. Unpin when dry.

Chart

Rnd 1: [K1, yo, k3, sk2po, k3, yo] to end.
Rnds 2, 4, 6, 8: K to end.
Rnd 3: [K2, yo, k2, sk2po, k2, yo, k1] to end.
Rnd 5: [Yo, ssk, k1, yo, k1, sk2po, k1, yo, k2] to end.
Rnd 7: [K1 tbl, yo, ssk, k1, yo, sk2po, yo, k1, k2tog, yo] to end.
Rnd 9: K to end.
Rnd 10: P to end.
Rnd 11: [K2tog, yo] to end.
Rnd 12: P to end.

Cast On

Using C2, CO 120 sts. Join to work in the round, being careful not to twist sts.
If you find it difficult to join to work in the round without twisting the cast-on round, work a few rows flat first, then join to work in the round. Make sure you convert any stitch pattern to work flat instead of in the round.

Edging

Rnd 1: Continuing with C2, p to end.
Rnd 2: K to end.
Rnd 3: P to end.
Rnd 4: [K2tog, yo] to end.
Rnd 5: P to end.

Work Chart A

Rnd 1: With C1, work Rnd 1 of Chart 12 times.
Rnd 2: Work Rnd 2 of Chart 12 times.

Chart

	10	9	8	7	6	5	4	3	2	1	
	•	•	•	•	•	•	•	•	•	•	12
	O	/	O	/	O	/	O	/	O	/	11
	•	•	•	•	•	•	•	•	•	•	10
											9
											8
	O	/		O	∧	O		\	O	Ω	7
											6
			O		∧		O		\	O	5
											4
		O			∧			O			3
											2
	O				∧				O		1

Key

☐	knit
O	yo
/	k2tog
\	ssk
Ω	k1 tbl
∧	sk2po
•	purl

Mykonos

These beautiful hand warmers are worked in the round using a beaded lace pattern and rib.

Finished Measurements

Hand Circumference: 7–9 in/17.5–23 cm
Length: 10 in/25.5 cm

Yarn

Opal Uni Solid 4 Ply, super fine weight #1 yarn, 75% wool/25% polyamide, 465 yd/425 m, 3.5 oz/100 g
- 1 ball #1990 Green

Needles and Other Materials

- US size 4 (3.5 mm) double-pointed needles (or a 32 in/80 cm long circular needle for the magic loop technique)
- 104 size 6 seed beads (shown in Debbie Abrahams color #605)
- US size 15 (0.5 mm) steel crochet hook
- Tapestry needle
- Waste yarn

Gauge

29 sts x 45½ rows in Chart patt, lightly stretched = 4 in/10 cm square
Be sure to check your gauge!

Special Stitches and Techniques

Sk2po: Slip 1 stitch knitwise, knit 2 stitches together, pass slipped stitch over the k2tog stitch.

Add beads using the crochet hook method (B): Place bead on the crochet hook, lift st off left needle using the crochet hook and slip the bead onto the st. Replace it on left needle and knit.

Sewn bind-off: Break the yarn, leaving a tail approximately three times the length of the bind-off edge. Using a blunt tapestry needle, *insert tapestry needle into first 2 sts purlwise, pull yarn all the way through leaving the sts on the knitting needle. Insert tapestry needle into first st again knitwise and slip this st off the knitting needle; rep from * to end.

SKILL LEVEL

Level 2

NOTES

- For longer hand warmers, work more repeats of the Chart.
- See photo tutorials on how to work the sewn bind-off on page 19 and how to add beads with a crochet hook on page 22.

Begin Hand Warmers

CO 46 sts. Join to work in the round, being careful not
    to twist sts.

*If you find it difficult to join to work in the round without
    twisting the cast-on round, work a few rows flat first,
    then join to work in the round. Make sure you convert
    any stitch pattern to work flat instead of in the round.*

Round 1: P to end.

Round 2: K to end.

Rep last 2 rounds once more.

Round 5: P to end.

Work Chart

Rnd 1: Work Rnd 1 of Chart, working the 13-st rep
    twice, p1, (k2, p2) four times, k2, p1.

Rnd 2: Work Rnd 2 of Chart, working the 13-st rep
    twice, p1, (k2, p2) four times, k2, p1.

Rnd 3: Work Rnd 3 of Chart, working the 13-st rep
    twice, p1, (k2, p2) four times, k2, p1.

Continue working through all 8 rounds of the Chart
    10 times.

Right-Hand Warmer Only

Rnd 1: Work Rnd 1 of Chart, working the 13-st rep
    twice, p1, k the next 6 sts in waste yarn, slip those
    same 6 sts back to left needle, continue in pattern as
    established to end, using the main yarn.

Left-Hand Warmer Only

Rnd 1: Work Rnd 1 of Chart, working the 13-st rep
    twice, p1, (k2, p2) three times, k the next 6 sts in
    waste yarn, slip those same 6 sts back to left needle,
    and continue in pattern as established to end, using
    the main yarn.

Both Hand Warmers

Continue working through all 8 rounds of Chart a fur-
    ther three times.

Next rnd: P to the end.

Next rnd: K to the end.

Rep the last 2 rnds once more.

Next rnd: P to the end.

Bind off using the sewn bind-off.

Thumbs

Undo the waste yarn, placing 6 sts from the top and bottom onto two needles.

Attach the working yarn and work in [k2, p2] rib patt across the bottom sts, pick up and k2 (these will be p2 on the next round) in the gap, work in [k2, p2] rib patt across the top sts, pick up and k2 (these will be p2 on the next round) in the gap. Join to work in the round. *16 sts.*

Continue in [k2, p2] rib pattern and work a total of 12 rounds.

Bind off using the sewn bind-off.

Finishing

Weave in all loose ends.

Rnd 1: [P1, yo, B, ssk, k5, k2tog, B, yo, p1] twice.
Rnds 2, 4, 6: [P1, k11, p1] twice.
Rnd 3: [P1, k1, yo, k1, ssk, k3, k2tog, k1, yo, k1, p1] twice.
Rnd 5: [P1, k2, yo, B, ssk, k1, k2tog, B, yo, k2, p1] twice.
Rnd 7: [P1, k3, yo, k1, sk2po, k1, yo, k3, p1] twice.
Rnd 8: [P1, k11, p1] twice.

Chart

| 13 | 12 | 11 | 10 | 9 | 8 | 7 | 6 | 5 | 4 | 3 | 2 | 1 | |

Rows (bottom to top): 1–8

Key

knit		sk2po	
yo		add bead and knit (B)	
k2tog		purl	
ssk			

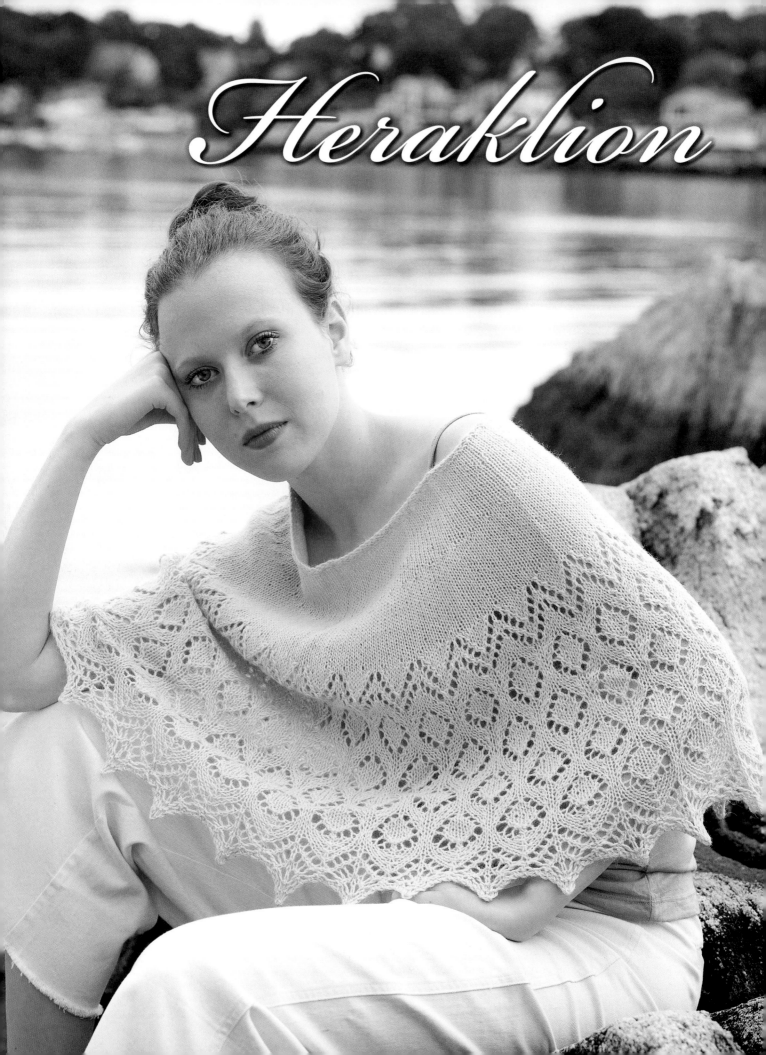

Heraklion

Heraklion is worked in a cozy, warm pure alpaca yarn. It looks perfect with jeans for a casual weekend look.

Finished Measurements

Sizes: Small (Medium, Large)
To Fit Bust: 34 (40, 46) in/86 (101.5, 116.5) cm
Neck Circumference: 30 (32^1/$_2$, 35) in/76 (82.5, 89) cm
Bind-Off Edge Circumference: 72 (88, 100) in/182.5 (223.5, 254) cm
Length: 20 (24, 28) in/50.5 (61, 71) cm

Yarn

Drops Alpaca, fine weight #2 yarn, 100% alpaca, 183 yd/167 m, 1.75 oz/50 g
- 4 (5, 6) balls #3112 Dusty Pink

Needles and Other Materials

- US size 4 (3.5 mm) circular needle, 16 in/40 cm long
- US size 6 (4 mm) circular needle, 32 in/80 cm long
- Tapestry needle
- Stitch markers

Gauge

22 sts x 24 rows in St st on smaller needles after blocking = 4 in/10 cm square
17 sts x 20^1/$_2$ rows in Chart B patt on larger needles after blocking = 4 in/10 cm square
Be sure to check your gauge!

Special Stitches and Techniques

Sk2po: Slip 1 stitch knitwise, knit 2 stitches together, pass slipped stitch over the k2tog stitch.

Russian bind-off: Knit 2 stitches. *Insert the left needle into the front of those 2 stitches and knit both stitches together (or slip both stitches back to the left needle and knit through back loop). This leaves 1 stitch on the right needle. Knit 1. Repeat from * until the correct number of stitches have been bound off. Once you've bound off the required stitches, you will be left with 1 stitch on your right needle. Break the yarn and pull it through this stitch as for a normal bind-off.

SKILL LEVEL

Level 2

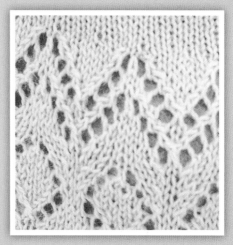

NOTES

- Heraklion is a poncho worked in the round from the top down. The shaping takes place in the stockinette section, which makes the lace section easier as there's no shaping to worry about.
- You can customize the length of your poncho: Make it longer by working more repeats of Chart A and/or B; make it shorter by working fewer repeats of Chart A and/or B.
- See page 17 for a photo tutorial on how to work the Russian bind-off.

Begin Poncho

Using a US size 4 (3.5 mm) circular needle, CO 120 (130, 140) sts.

Join to work in the round, being careful not to twist sts.

If you find it difficult to join to work in the round without twisting the cast-on round, work a few rows flat first, then join to work in the round. Make sure you convert any stitch pattern to work flat instead of work in the round.

Rnd 1: P to end.
Rnd 2: K to end.
Rnd 3: P to end.

Next rnd:
Size Small: [(K2, m1, k3, m1) twice, k2, m1] 10 times. *170 sts*
Size Medium: [(K3, m1, k2, m1) twice, k3, m1] 10 times. *180 sts*
Size Large: [K2, m1, (k3, m1) four times] 10 times. *190 sts*

Continue in St st (knit all sts) until the poncho measures 3 (3½, 4) in/7.5 (9, 10) cm.

Next rnd:
Size Small: [K4, m1, (k3, m1) 10 times] five times. *225 sts.*
Size Medium: [K3, m1, (k2, m1) three times] 20 times. *260 sts.*
Size Large: [(K1, m1) four times, (k2, m1) 17 times] five times. *295 sts.*

Continue in St st until the poncho measures 6 (7, 8) in/15 (18, 20.5) cm.

Next rnd:
Size Small: [K5, m1, (k4, m1) 10 times] five times. *280 sts.*
Size Medium: [(K3, m1) three times, k4, m1] 20 times. *340 sts.*
Size Large: [(K2, m1) four times, (k3, m1) 17 times] five times. *400 sts.*

Change to US size 6 (4 mm) needles.

Work Chart A

Rnd 1: Work Rnd 1 of Chart A 28 (34, 40) times.
Rnd 2: Work Rnd 2 of Chart A 28 (34, 40) times.
Continue working through all 12 rnds of Chart A one (two, three) times.

Work Chart B

Rnd 1: Work Rnd 1 of Chart B 28 (34, 40) times.
Rnd 2: Work Rnd 2 of Chart B 28 (34, 40) times.
Continue working through all 24 rnds of Chart B twice.

Work Chart C

Rnd 1: Work Rnd 1 of Chart C 28 (34, 40) times.
Rnd 2: Work Rnd 2 of Chart C 28 (34, 40) times.
Continue working through all 12 rounds of Chart C once.

Bind off using the Russian bind-off.

Finishing

Weave in loose ends. Soak the poncho in lukewarm water. Squeeze out excess water in a towel. Stretch the poncho to size and shape and pin in place. Leave to dry.

Chart A

Pattern repeat is indicated by [ ].

Rnd 1: [K1, yo, ssk, k5, k2tog, yo] to end.

Rnd 2 and all even-numbered rounds: K to end.

Rnd 3: [K2, yo, ssk, k3, k2tog, yo, k1] to end.

Rnd 5: [K1, (yo, ssk) twice, k1, (k2tog, yo) twice] to end.

Rnd 7: [K2, yo, ssk, yo, sk2po, yo, k2tog, yo, k1] to end.

Rnd 9: [K3, yo, ssk, k1, k2tog, yo, k2] to end.

Rnd 11: [K4, yo, sk2po, yo, k3] to end.

Rnd 12: K to end.

Chart B

Note: On Rnd 10, move the last st (in green) to the begin-ning of the next round.

Pattern repeat is indicated by [ ].

Rnd 1: [K1, yo, k2, ssk, k1, k2tog, k2, yo] to end.

Rnd 2 and all even-numbered rnds (except Rnd 10): K to end.

Rnd 3: [K2, yo, k1, ssk, k1, k2tog, k1, yo, k1] to end.

Rnd 5: [K3, yo, ssk, k1, k2tog, yo, k2] to end.

Rnd 7: [K2, k2tog, yo, k3, yo, ssk, k1] to end.

Rnd 9: [K1, k2tog, yo, k5, yo, ssk] to end.

Rnd 10: K to last st, move m before last st; this st becomes first st in Rnd 11.

Rnd 11: [Sk2po, yo, k7, yo] to end.

Rnd 13: [K1, k2tog, k2, yo, k1, yo, k2, ssk] to end.

Rnd 15: [K1, k2tog, k1, yo, k3, yo, k1, ssk] to end.

Rnd 17: [K1, k2tog, yo, k5, yo, ssk] to end.

Rnd 19: [K2, yo, ssk, k3, k2tog, yo, k1] to end.

Rnd 21: [K3, yo, ssk, k1, k2tog, yo, k2] to end.

Rnd 23: [K4, yo, sk2po, yo, k3] to end.

Rnd 24: K to end.

Chart C

Pattern repeat is indicated by [ ].

Rnd 1: [K1, yo, k3, sk2po, k3, yo] to end.

Rnds 2, 4, 6, and 8: K to end.

Rnd 3: [K2, yo, k2, sk2po, k2, yo, k1] to end.

Rnd 5: [K1, yo, ssk, yo, k1, sk2po, k1, yo, k2tog, yo] to end.

Rnd 7: [K2, yo, ssk, yo, sk2po, yo, k2tog, yo, k1] to end.

Rnd 9: [K1, (yo, ssk) twice, k1, (k2tog, yo) twice] to end.

Rnd 10: P to end.

Rnd 11: [K2, yo, ssk, yo, sk2po, yo, k2tog, yo, k1] to end.

Rnd 12: P to end.

Chart A

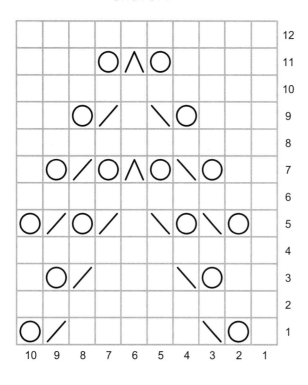

Chart C

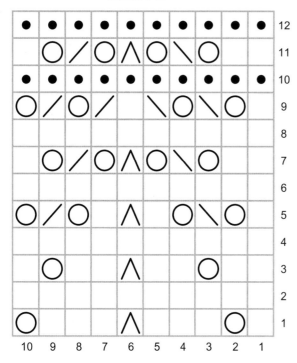

Chart B

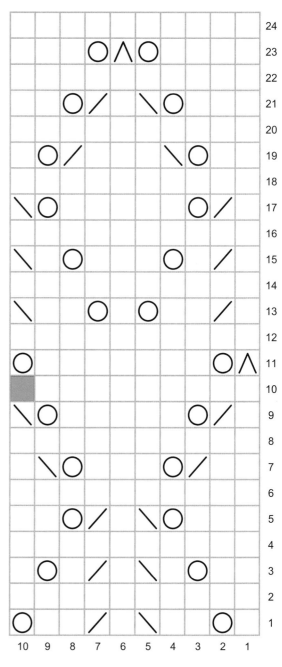

Key

☐	knit	╲	ssk
◯	yo	⋀	sk2po
╱	k2tog	●	purl
╲	ssk	▨	Move marker before this stitch on Rnd 10, which becomes 1st st in Rnd 11

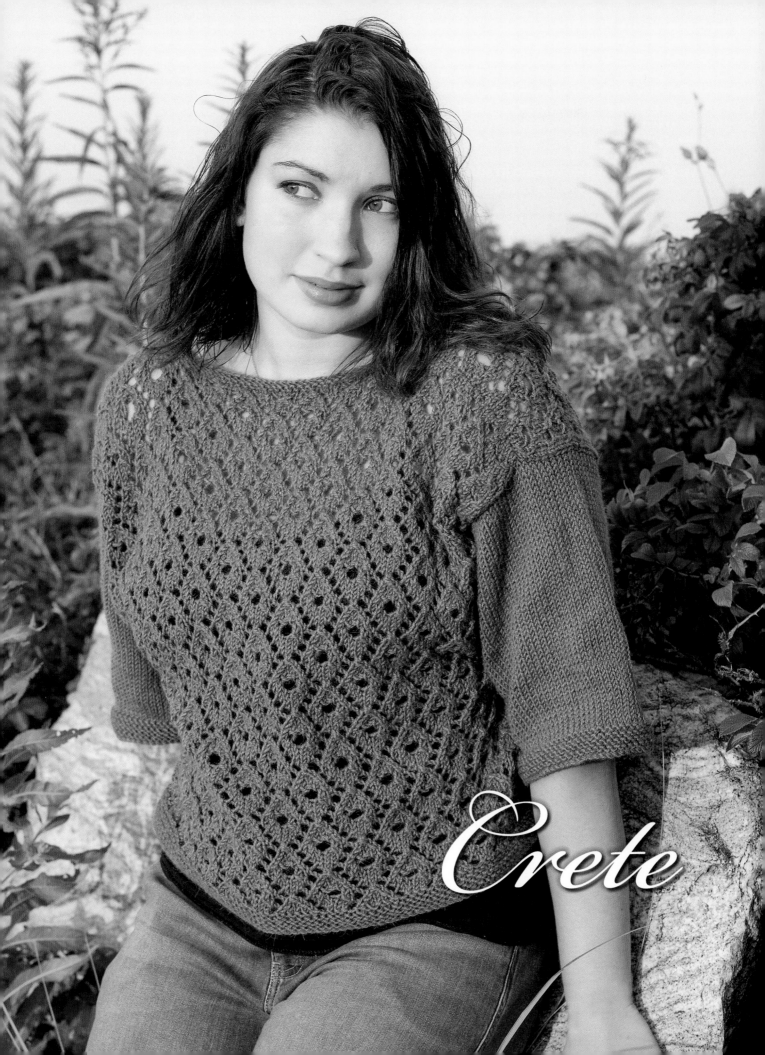

Crete

Crete is a simple sweater with an oversized silhouette. The body is worked in lace, and the sleeves are worked in stockinette stitch.

SKILL LEVEL

Level 2

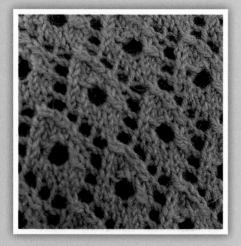

NOTES

- When measuring the lace while knitting, stretch the piece to simulate blocking.
- See pages 18 and 19 for a photo tutorial on how to work the three-needle bind-off.

Finished Measurements

Sizes: Small (Medium, Large, 1X, 2X)
To Fit Bust: 34 (38, 42, 46, 50) in/86 (96.5, 106.5, 116.5, 127) cm
Actual Bust: 46 (52, 57, 63, 68) in/116.5 (132, 144.5, 160, 172.5) cm
Length: 21 (22, 23, 24, 24½) in/53 (55.5, 58.5, 61, 62) cm
Sleeve Length: 10 (10½, 10¾, 11, 11¾) in/25.5 (26.5, 27, 28, 29.5) cm

Yarn

Berroco Ultra Alpaca, medium weight #4 yarn, 50% super fine alpaca/50% Peruvian wool, 215 yd/198 m, 3.5 oz/100 g
- 5 (5, 6, 7, 8) skeins #62112 Concord Grape

Needles and Other Materials

- US size 7 (4.5 mm) needles
- US size 7 (4.5 mm) circular needle, 16 in/40 cm long
- Tapestry needle
- 2 locking stitch markers

Gauge

15 sts x 24 rows in Chart patt after blocking = 4 in/10 cm square
18 sts x 26 rows in St st after blocking = 4 in/10 cm square
Be sure to check your gauge!

Special Stitches and Techniques

Sk2po: Slip 1 stitch knitwise, knit 2 stitches together, pass slipped stitch over the k2tog stitch.

Three-needle bind-off: Hold the two pieces to be joined, each on a separate needle, in your left hand with right sides together. Insert the third needle into the first stitch on the back needle and the first stitch on the front needle purlwise and purl these 2 stitches together. Repeat on the next stitches, so you now have 2 stitches on the right needle. Lift the first stitch over the second stitch as in a regular bind-off. Repeat until all stitches have been bound off.

Back

CO 88 (98, 108, 118, 128) sts.
Row 1 (RS): K to end.
Row 2 (WS): K to end.
Rep last 2 rows a further three times (8 rows worked).

Work Lace Pattern

Row 1 (RS): Work Row 1 of the Chart, working the 10-st rep 8 (9, 10, 11, 12) times.
Row 2 (WS): Work Row 2 of the Chart, working the 10-st rep 8 (9, 10, 11, 12) times.
Continue working through all rows of the Chart until the back measures 20½ (21½, 22½, 23½, 24) in/52 (54.5, 57, 59.5, 61) cm.

Shape Right Neck

Row 1 (RS): Work 30 (35, 39, 44, 48) sts in pattern, turn.
Row 2 (WS): P1, p2tog, work in pattern to end. *1 st dec.*
Row 3: Work in pattern to last 3 sts, k2tog, k1. *1 st dec. 28 (33, 37, 42, 46) sts.*
Leave sts on hold.

Shape Left Neck

Leave 28 (28, 30, 30, 32) sts on hold for back neck. Reattach yarn at neck edge.
Row 1 (RS): Work in pattern to end. *30 (35, 39, 44, 48) sts.*
Row 2 (WS): Work in pattern to last 3 sts, p2tog tbl, p1. *1 st dec.*
Row 3: K1, ssk, work in pattern to end. *1 st dec. 28 (33, 37, 42, 46) sts.*
Leave sts on hold.

Front

CO 88 (98, 108, 118, 128) sts.
Row 1 (RS): K to end.
Row 2 (WS): K to end.
Rep last 2 rows three more times (8 rows worked).

Work Lace Pattern

Row 1 (RS): Work Row 1 of the Chart, working the 10-st rep 8 (9, 10, 11, 12) times.
Row 2 (WS): Work Row 2 of the Chart, working the 10-st rep 8 (9, 10, 11, 12) times.

Leave 24 (24, 26, 26, 28) sts on hold for front neck. Reattach yarn at neck edge.

Row 1 (RS): Work in pattern to end. *32 (37, 41, 46, 50) sts.*

Row 2 (WS): Work in pattern to last 3 sts, p2tog tbl, p1. *1 st dec.*

Row 3: K1, ssk, work in pattern to end. *1 st dec.*

Rep last 2 rows once more. *28 (33, 37, 42, 46) sts.*

Work until right front matches back to shoulder.

Leave sts on hold.

Sleeve (make 2)

CO 68 (70, 74, 78, 80) sts.

Row 1 (RS): K to end.

Row 2 (WS): K to end.

Rep last 2 rows three more times (8 rows worked).

Row 1 (RS): K to end.

Row 2 (WS): P to end.

Rep last two rows once more.

Next row (RS): K2, m1, k to last 2 sts, m1, k2. *2 sts inc.*

Work 3 (3, 3, 3, 3) rows in St st.

Next row (RS): K2, m1, k to last 2 sts, m1, k2. *2 sts inc.*

Rep the last 4 rows a further 9 (9, 9, 9, 11) times. *90 (92, 96, 100, 106) sts.*

Continue in St st until sleeve measures 10 (10½, 10¾, 11, 11¾) in/25.5 (26.5, 27.5, 28, 30) cm.

Place a locking st marker in the center of the row. Bind off all sts.

Finishing

Block pieces to measurements.

Join the shoulders by working a three-needle bind-off on the WS.

Line up the marker on the center top sleeve with the shoulder seam and seam the sleeves to the shoulders. Seam side seams and sleeve seams.

Neck

Using the short circular needle and starting at the left shoulder with the RS facing, pick up and k14 (16, 18, 20, 22) to front neck, k24 (24, 26, 26, 28) from front

---

Continue working through all rows of the Chart until the front measures 18 (18½, 19, 19½, 19½) in/45.5 (47, 48, 49.5, 49.5) cm

Row 1 (RS): Work 32 (37, 41, 46, 50) sts in patt, turn. Leave rem sts on hold.

Row 2 (WS): P1, p2tog, work in pattern to end. *1 st dec.*

Row 3: Work in pattern to last 3 sts, k2tog, k1. *1 st dec.*

Rep last 2 rows once more. *28 (33, 37, 42, 46) sts.*

Work until left front matches back to shoulder.

Leave sts on hold.

neck, pick up and k14 (16, 18, 20, 22) to right shoulder, pick up and k3 to back neck, k28 (28, 30, 30, 32) from back neck, pick up and k3 to left shoulder. Join to work in the round. Place a marker to mark beg of round. 86 (90, 98, 102, 110) sts.

Rnd 1: P to end.
Rnd 2: K to end.
Rnd 3: P to end.
Rnd 4: K to end.
Bind off purlwise.
Weave in all loose ends.

Chart

Pattern repeat is in [ ].
Row 1 (RS): K4, [k1 tbl, k2tog, yo, k3, yo, ssk, k1 tbl, k1] to last 4 sts, k4.
Row 2 (WS): Purl to end.
Row 3: K4, [k2tog, yo, k5, yo, ssk, k1] to last 4 sts, k4.
Row 4: Purl to end.
Row 5: K2, yo, sk2po, [yo, k1, sk2po, (yo) three times, k2tog, k1, yo, sk2po] to last 3 sts, yo, k3.
Row 6: P4, [p5, p1 tbl, p4] to last 4 sts, p4.
Row 7: K4, [k1, yo, ssk, k1 tbl, k1, k1 tbl, k2tog, yo, k2] to last 4 sts, k4.
Row 8: Purl to end.
Row 9: K4, [k2, yo, ssk, k1, k2tog, yo, k3] to last 4 sts, k4.
Row 10: Purl to end.
Row 11: K2, k2tog, yo, [yo, k2tog, k1 tbl, yo, sk2po, yo, k1, sk2po, (yo) twice] to last 4 sts, yo, k2tog, k2.
Row 12: P4, [p1 tbl, p9] to last 4 sts, p1 tbl, p3.

Chart

Key

□	RS: knit WS: purl
○	RS: yo
∧	RS: sk2po
╱	RS: k2tog
╲	RS: ssk
Ω	RS: k tbl WS: p tbl
□	pattern repeat

Ibiza

This beautiful shawl converts into a shrug with the addition of two buttons. Ibiza is lightweight and easier than it looks.

Finished Measurements

Wingspan: 56 in/142 cm
Depth: 22 in/56 cm

Yarn

Schoppel Wolle 6 Karat, lace weight #0 yarn, 80% extra-fine virgin wool/ 20% silk, 656 yd/600 m, 3.5 oz/100 g
- 1 skein #2287 Meeresblick (Sea View)

Needles and Other Materials

- US size 5 (3.75 mm) circular needle, 32 in/80 cm long
- Two 1 in/2.5 cm buttons (optional)
- Tapestry needle
- 2 locking stitch markers (optional)

Gauge

20 sts x 24 rows in Chart B patt after blocking = 4 in/10 cm square
Be sure to check your gauge!

Special Stitches and Techniques

Sk2po: Slip 1 stitch knitwise, knit 2 stitches together, pass the slipped stitch over the k2tog stitch.

Russian bind-off: Knit 2 stitches. *Insert the left needle into the front of those 2 stitches and knit both stitches together (or slip both stitches back to the left needle and knit through back loop). This leaves 1 stitch on the right needle. Knit 1. Repeat from * until the correct number of stitches have been bound off. Once you've bound off the required stitches, you will be left with 1 stitch on your right needle. Break the yarn and pull it through this stitch as for a normal bind-off.

SKILL LEVEL

Level 2

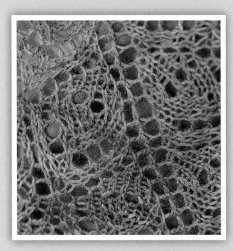

NOTES

- You may wish to put a locking stitch marker on the stitches in bold, which indicate the spines. You will increase on either side of both spines as well as inside the first 2 and the last 2 stitches. Placing locking stitch markers on the spine stitches will help you remember to increase as directed and keep your place in the pattern.
- Charts show RS rows only; see pattern for WS rows.
- See page 17 for a photo tutorial on how to work the Russian bind-off.

Cast On

CO 9 sts. Knit 1 row.

Stockinette Stitch Section

I recommend placing locking stitch markers on the stitches in bold to help you keep your place in the pattern. Move these markers up every few rows.

Row 1: K2, (yo, k1) to last 2 sts, yo, k2. *6 sts inc.*

Row 2 (WS and all following WS rows): K2, p to last 2 sts, k2.

Row 3: K2, (yo, k3, yo, **k1**) twice, yo, k3, yo, k2. *6 sts inc.*

Row 5: K2, (yo, k5, yo, **k1**) twice, yo, k5, yo, k2. *6 sts inc.*

Row 7: K2, (yo, k7, yo, **k1**) twice, yo, k7, yo, k2. *6 sts inc.*

Row 9: K2, (yo, k9, yo, **k1**) twice, yo, k9, yo, k2. *6 sts inc.*

Row 11: K2, (yo, k11, yo, **k1**) twice, yo, k11, yo, k2. *6 sts inc. 45 sts.*

Row 12: K2, p to last 2 sts, k2.

Work Chart A

Row 1 (RS): K2, (work Row 1 of Chart A, **k1**) twice, work Row 1 of Chart A, k2. *6 sts inc.*

Row 2 (WS and all following WS rows): K2, p to last 2 sts, k2.

Row 3: K2, (work Row 3 of Chart A, **k1**) twice, work Row 3 of Chart A, k2. *6 sts inc.*

Continue working through all 12 rows of Chart A. *81 sts.*

Work Chart B

Row 1 (RS): K2, (work Row 1 of Chart B, working the 12-st rep once, **k1**) twice, work Row 1 of Chart B, working the 12-st rep once, k2. *6 sts inc.*

Row 2 (WS and all following WS rows): K2, p to last 2 sts, k2.

Row 3: K2, (work Row 3 of Chart B, working the 12-st rep once, **k1**) twice, work Row 3 of Chart B, working the 12-st rep once, k2. *6 sts inc.*

Continue working through all 12 rows of Chart B a total of nine times. For each 12-row repeat, work another 12-stitch repeat. *405 sts.*

Work Chart C

Row 1: K2, (work Row 1 of Chart C, working the 12-st rep 10 times, **k1**) twice, work Row 1 of Chart C, working the 12-st rep 10 times, k2. *6 sts inc.*

Row 2 (WS and all following WS rows): K2, p to last 2 sts, k2.

Row 3: K2, (work Row 3 of Chart C, working the 12-st rep 10 times, **k1**) twice, work Row 3 of Chart C, working the 12-st rep 10 times, k2. *6 sts inc.*

Continue working through all 12 rows of Chart C once. *441 sts.*

Bind off using the Russian bind-off.

Finishing

Weave in all loose ends. Soak the shawl in lukewarm water. Squeeze out excess water. Stretch the shawl to size and shape and pin in place. Leave to dry. Unpin when dry.

To wear as a shrug: On the WS, attach buttons to the bottom of each spine. Fold the front edges over and fasten the buttons through a yarn over.

Chart A

Row 1 (RS): Yo, k3, yo, k2, sk2po, k2, yo, k3, yo.

Row 2 (WS and all following WS rows): K2, p to last 2 sts, k2.

Row 3: Yo, k2, yo, k1, ssk, yo, k1, sk2po, k1, yo, k2tog, k1, yo, k2, yo.

Row 5: Yo, k4, yo, k1, ssk, yo, sk2po, yo, k2tog, k1, yo, k4, yo.

Row 7: Yo, k6, yo, k1, ssk, k1, k2tog, k1, yo, k6, yo.

Row 9: Yo, k2, k2tog, yo, k1, yo, ssk, k1, yo, k1, sk2po, k1, yo, k1, k2tog, yo, k1, yo, ssk, k2, yo.

Row 11: Yo, k10, yo, sk2po, yo, k10, yo.

Row 12: K2, p to last 2 sts, k2.

Chart B

Pattern repeat is in [ ]. For each 12-row repeat, work an additional 12-st repeat.

Row 1 (RS): Yo, k3, yo, k2, [sk2po, k2, yo, k5, yo, k2] once, sk2po, k2, yo, k3, yo.

Row 2 (WS and all following WS rows): K2, p to last 2 sts, k2.

Row 3: Yo, k2, yo, k1, ssk, yo, k1, [sk2po, k1, yo, k2tog, (k1, yo) twice, k1, ssk, yo, k1] once, sk2po, k1, yo, k2tog, k1, yo, k2, yo.

Row 5: Yo, k4, yo, k1, ssk, yo, [sk2po, yo, k2tog, k1, yo, k3, yo, k1, ssk, yo] once, k1, yo, k2tog, k1, yo, k4, yo.

Row 7: Yo, k6, yo, k1, ssk, [k1, k2tog, k1, yo, k5, yo, k1, ssk] once, k1, k2tog, k1, yo, k6, yo.

Row 9: Yo, k2, k2tog, yo, k1, yo, ssk, k1, yo, k1, [sk2po, k1, yo, k1, k2tog, yo, k1, yo, ssk, k1, yo, k1] once, sk2po, k1, yo, k1, k2tog, yo, k1, yo, ssk, k2, yo.

Row 11: Yo, k10, yo, [sk2po, yo, k9, yo] once, sk2po, yo, k10, yo.

Row 12: K2, p to last 2 sts, k2.

Chart C

Pattern repeat is in [ ].

Row 1 (RS): Yo, k2tog, k2, yo, k2, [k3, yo, k2, sk2po, k2, yo, k2] 10 times, k3, yo, k2, ssk, yo.

Row 2 (WS and all WS rows): K2, p to last 2 sts, k2.

Row 3: Yo, k1, (k2tog, k1, yo) twice, [k1, yo, k1, ssk, yo, k1, sk2po, k1, yo, k2tog, k1, yo] 10 times, k1, (yo, k1, ssk) twice, k1, yo.

Row 5: Yo, k2, k2tog, yo, k2tog, k1, yo, k1, [k2, yo, k1, ssk, yo, sk2po, yo, k2tog, k1, yo, k1] 10 times, k2, yo, k1, ssk, yo, ssk, k2, yo.

Row 7: Yo, k4, k2tog, k1, yo, k2tog, yo, [k1, yo, ssk, yo, k1, ssk, k1, k2tog, k1, yo, k2tog, yo] 10 times, k1, yo, ssk, yo, k1, ssk, k4, yo.

Row 9: Yo, k2, yo, k1, sk2po, k1, yo, k2tog, yo, k1, [k2, yo, ssk, yo, k1, sk2po, k1, yo, k2tog, yo, k1] 10 times, k2, yo, ssk, yo, k1, sk2po, k1, yo, k2, yo.

Row 11: Yo, k2, yo, ssk, yo, sk2po, (yo, k2tog) twice, yo, [k1, (yo, ssk) twice, yo, sk2po, (yo, k2tog) twice, yo] 10 times, k1, (yo, ssk) twice, yo, sk2po, yo, k2tog, yo, k2, yo.

Row 12: K2, p to last 2 sts, k2.

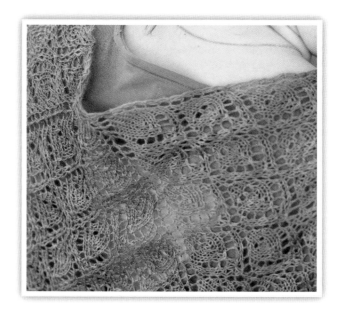

Key

☐	RS: knit
◯	RS: yo
╱	RS: k2tog
╲	RS: ssk
⋀	RS: sk2po
☐	pattern repeat

Chart A

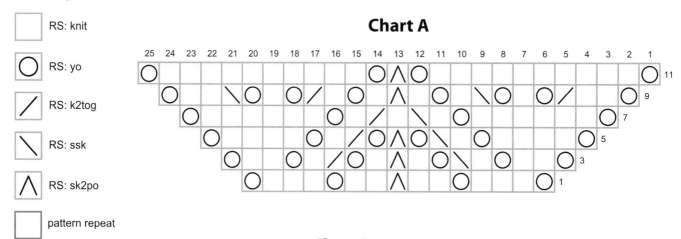

Chart B

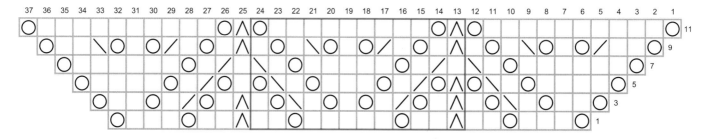

Chart C

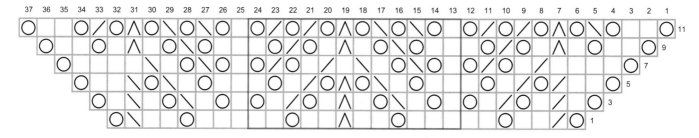

Valencia

Valencia is a classic triangle shawl worked from the top down. You begin by working in stockinette stitch while you get used to the shaping, and then you'll add the interesting lace pattern.

SKILL LEVEL

Level 3

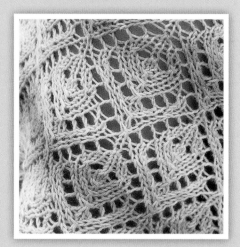

NOTES

- Charts show RS rows only; see pattern for WS rows.
- See page XX for a photo tutorial on how to work the Russian bind-off.

Finished Measurements

Wingspan: 60 in/152.5 cm
Depth: 33 in/84 cm

Yarn

Schachenmayr Fashion Tahiti, super fine weight #1 yarn, 99% cotton/1% polyester, 306 yd/280 m, 1.75 oz/50 g
- 2 skeins #07652 Aquatic

Needles and Other Materials

- US size 6 (4 mm) needles (32 in/80 cm circular needle is recommended)
- Tapestry needle
- Stitch holder or waste yarn
- Locking stitch marker (optional)

Gauge

17 sts x 24 rows in Chart A patt after blocking = 4 in/10 cm square
Be sure to check your gauge!

Special Stitches and Techniques

Sk2po: Slip 1 stitch knitwise, knit 2 stitches together, pass the slipped stitch over the k2tog stitch.

Russian bind-off (RBO): Knit 2 stitches. *Insert the left needle into the front of those 2 stitches and knit both stitches together (or slip both stitches back to the left needle and knit through back loop). This leaves 1 stitch on the right needle. Knit 1. Repeat from * until the correct number of stitches have been bound off. Once you've bound off the required stitches, you will be left with 1 stitch on your right needle. Break the yarn and pull it through this stitch as for a normal bind-off.

Cast On

CO 9 sts. Knit 1 row.

Stockinette Stitch Section

Row 1 (RS): Sl wyif, k2, (yo, k1) three times, yo, k3. *4 sts inc.*

Row 2 (WS and all following WS rows): Sl wyif, k2, p to last 3 sts, k3.

I recommend placing a locking stitch marker on the stitch in bold. This will become the central spine st. Move the marker up every few rows.

Row 3: Sl wyif, k2, yo, k3, yo, **k1**, yo, k3, yo, k3. *4 sts inc.*

Row 5: Sl wyif, k2, yo, k to marked st, yo, **k1**, yo, k to last 3 sts, yo, k3. *4 sts inc.*

Continue as established, increasing 4 stitches every other row, for a total of 60 rows. *129 sts.*

Work Chart A

Row 1 (RS): Sl wyif, k2, work Row 1 of Chart A, working the 12-st rep four times, to marked st, **k1**, work Row 1 of Chart A, working the 12-st rep four times, to last 3 sts, k3. *4 sts inc.*

Row 2 (WS and all following WS rows): Sl wyif, k2, p to last 3 sts, k3.

Row 3: Sl wyif, k2, work Row 3 of Chart A, working the 12-st rep four times, to marked st, **k1**, work Row 3 of Chart A, working the 12-st rep four times, to last 3 sts, k3. *4 sts inc.*

Continue working through all 12-row repeats of Chart A a total of nine times. For each subsequent 12-row rep of Chart A, work another 12-st rep in each half. *345 sts.*

Work Chart B

Row 1 (RS): Sl wyif, k2, work Row 1 of Chart B, working the 12-st rep 13 times, to marked st, **k1**, work Row 1 of Chart B, working the 12-st rep 13 times, to last 3 sts, k3. *4 sts inc.*

Row 2 (WS and all following WS rows): Sl wyif, k2, p to last 3 sts, k3.

Row 3: Sl wyif, k2, work Row 3 of Chart B, working the 12-st rep 13 times, to marked st, **k1**, work Row 3 of

Chart B, working the 12-st rep 13 times, to last 3 sts, k3. *4 sts inc.*

Continue working through all 12 rows of Chart B once. *369 sts.*

Finishing

Weave in all loose ends. Soak the shawl in lukewarm water. Squeeze out excess water. Stretch the shawl to size and shape and pin in place. Leave to dry. Unpin when dry.

Chart A

For each subsequent 12-row repeat, work another 12-st repeat in each half.

Pattern repeat is indicated by [ ].

Row 1 (RS): Yo, k3, yo, k2, [sk2po, k2, yo, k5, yo, k2] four times, sk2po, k2, yo, k3, yo.

Row 2 (WS and all following WS rows): Sl wyif, k2, p to last 3 sts, k3.

Row 3: Yo, k2, yo, k1, ssk, yo, k1, [sk2po, k1, yo, k2tog, (k1, yo) twice, k1, ssk, yo, k1] four times, sk2po, k1, yo, k2tog, k1, yo, k2, yo.

Row 5: Yo, k4, yo, k1, ssk, yo, [sk2po, yo, k2tog, k1, yo, k3, yo, k1, ssk, yo] four times, sk2po, yo, k2tog, k1, yo, k4, yo.

Row 7: Yo, k6, yo, k1, ssk, [k1, k2tog, k1, yo, k5, yo, k1, ssk] four times, k1, k2tog, k1, yo, k6, yo.

Row 9: Yo, k2, k2tog, yo, k1, yo, ssk, k1, yo, k1, [sk2po, k1, yo, k1, k2tog, yo, k1, yo, ssk, k1, yo, k1] four times, sk2po, k1, yo, k1, k2tog, yo, k1, yo, ssk, k2, yo.

Row 11: Yo, k10, yo, [sk2po, yo, k9, yo] four times, sk2po, yo, k10, yo.

Row 12: Sl wyif, k2, p to last 3 sts, k3.

Chart B

Pattern repeat is indicated by [ ].

Row 1 (RS): Yo, k3, yo, k2, [sk2po, k2, yo, k5, yo, k2] 13 times, sk2po, k2, yo, k3, yo.

Row 2 (WS and all following WS rows): Sl wyif, k2, p to last 3 sts, k3.

Row 3: Yo, k2, yo, k1, ssk, yo, k1, [sk2po, k1, yo, k2tog, (k1, yo) twice, k1, ssk, yo, k1] 13 times, sk2po, k1, yo, k2tog, k1, yo, k2, yo.

Row 5: Yo, k4, yo, k1, ssk, yo, [sk2po, yo, k2tog, k1, yo, k3, yo, k1, ssk, yo] 13 times, sk2po, yo, k2tog, k1, yo, k4, yo.

Row 7: Yo, k1, k2tog, yo, k1, yo, ssk, yo, k1, ssk, [k1, k2tog, k1, yo, k2tog, yo, k1, yo, ssk, yo, k1, ssk] 13 times, k1, k2tog, k1, yo, k2tog, yo, k1, yo, ssk, k1, yo.

Row 9: Yo, k1, k2tog, yo, k3, yo, ssk, yo, k1, [sk2po, k1, yo, k2tog, yo, k3, yo, ssk, yo, k1] 13 times, sk2po, k1, yo, k2tog, yo, k3, yo, ssk, k1, yo.

Row 11: Yo, k1, (k2tog, yo) twice, k1, (yo, ssk) twice, yo, [sk2po, (yo, k2tog) twice, yo, k1, (yo, ssk) twice, yo] 13 times, sk2po, (yo, k2tog) twice, yo, k1, (yo, ssk) twice, k1, yo.

Row 12: Sl wyif, k2, p to last 3 sts, k3.

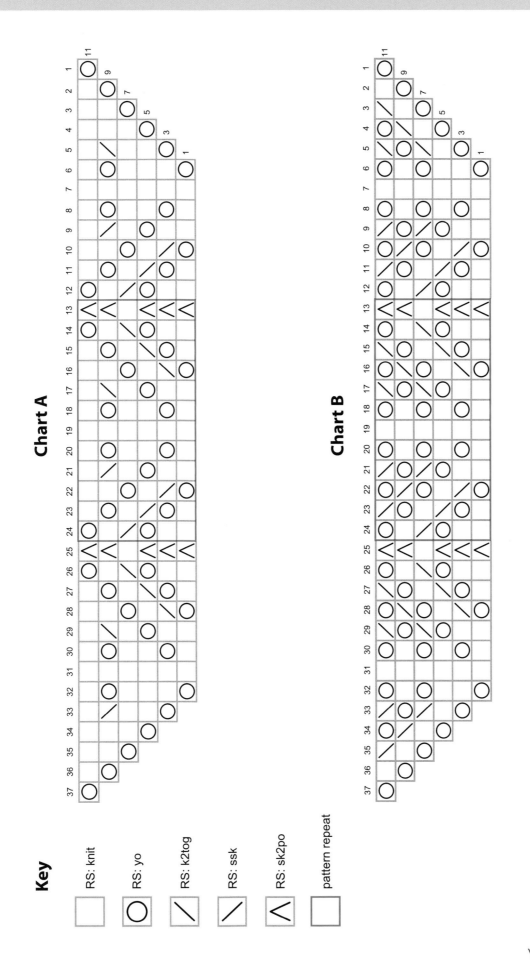

Chart A

Chart B

Key

☐	RS: knit
◯	RS: yo
╱	RS: k2tog
╱	RS: ssk
⋀	RS: sk2po
☐	pattern repeat

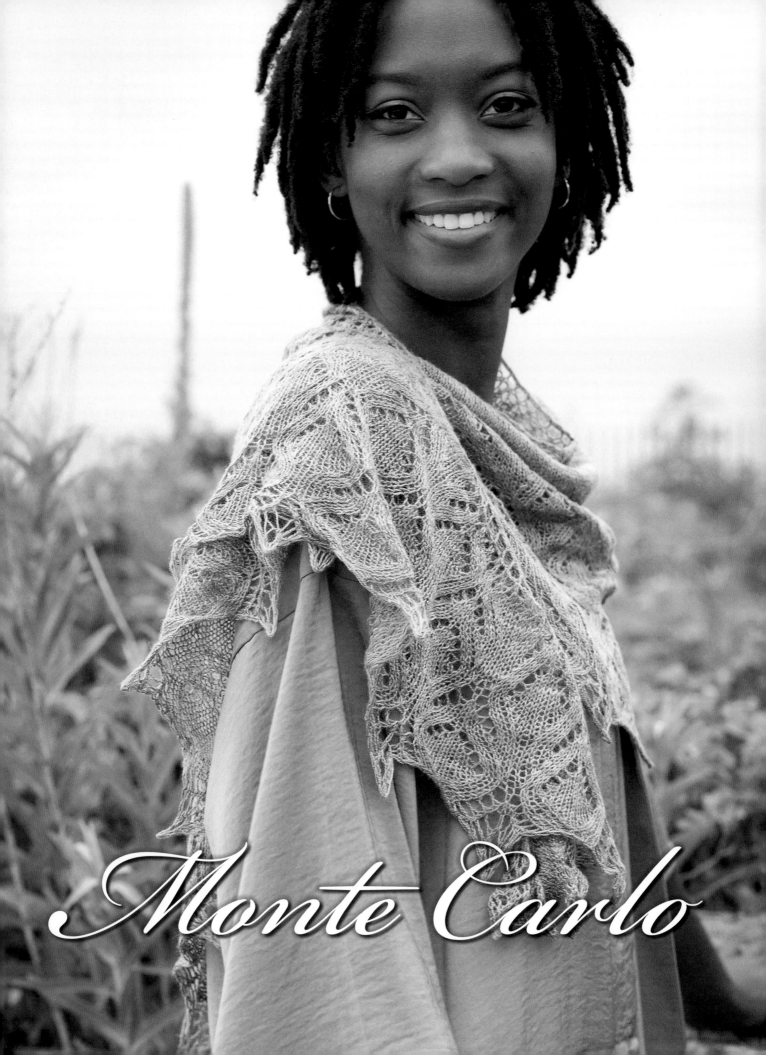

Monte Carlo

onte Carlo is a delicate, luxurious crescent shawl worked from the top down. It is light as air and perfect to wear over a pretty dress for a night out or over a sundress on a cool summer day. Monte Carlo starts with stockinette stitch to allow you to get used to the shaping before you start the lace pattern.

Finished Measurements

Wingspan: 61 in/155 cm
Depth: 17 in/43 cm

Yarn

Juniper Moon Farm Findley Dappled, super fine weight #1 yarn, 50% merino wool/50% silk, 798 yd/730 m, 3.5 oz/100 g
- 1 skein #120 Lime/Pink/Blue

Needles and Other Materials

- US size 4 (3.5 mm) circular needle, 32 in/80 cm long
- Tapestry needle

Gauge

20 sts x 26 rows in Chart A patt after blocking = 4 in/10 cm square
Be sure to check your gauge!

Special Stitches and Techniques

Sk2po: Slip 1 stitch knitwise, knit 2 stitches together, pass slipped stitch over the k2tog stitch.

Russian bind-off: Knit 2 stitches. *Insert the left needle into the front of those 2 stitches and knit both stitches together (or slip both stitches back to the left needle and knit through back loop). This leaves 1 stitch on the right needle. Knit 1. Repeat from * until the correct number of stitches have been bound off. Once you've bound off the required stitches, you will be left with 1 stitch on your right needle. Break the yarn and pull it through this stitch as for a normal bind-off.

SKILL LEVEL

Level 3

NOTES

- For a photo tutorial on how to work the Russian bind-off, see page 17.
- Charts show RS rows only; see pattern for WS rows.

Cast On

CO 9 sts. Knit 1 row.

Stockinette Stitch Section

Row 1 (RS): Sl wyif, (k1, yo) six times, k2. *6 sts inc. 15 sts.*

Row 2 (WS and all following WS rows): Sl wyif, k1, p to last 2 sts, k2.

Row 3: Sl wyif, (k1, yo) three times, k to last 4 sts, (yo, k1) three times, k1. *6 sts inc. 21 sts.*

Continue working as established, increasing 6 sts every other row for a total of 54 rows. *171 sts.*

Work Chart A

Row 1 (RS): Work Row 1 of Chart A, working the 16-st rep 10 times. *6 sts inc.*

Row 2 (WS and all following WS rows): Sl wyif, k1, p to last 2 sts, k2.

Row 3: Work Row 3 of Chart A, working the 16-st rep 10 times. *6 sts inc.*

Continue working through all 16 rows of Chart A for a total of five times. For each 16-row rep, work another three 16-st reps. *411 sts.*

Work Chart B

Row 1 (RS): Work Row 1 of Chart B, working the 16-st rep 25 times. *6 sts inc.*

Row 2 (WS and all following WS rows): Sl wyif, k1, p to last 2 sts, k2.

Row 3: Work Row 3 of Chart B, working the 16-st rep 25 times. *6 sts inc.*

Continue working through all 10 rows of Chart B once. *441 sts.*

Bind off using the Russian bind-off.

Finishing

Weave in all loose ends. Soak the shawl in lukewarm water. Squeeze out excess water. Stretch the shawl to size and shape and pin in place. Leave to dry. Unpin when dry.

Chart A

Pattern repeat is in [ ].

For each 16-row rep, work another three 16-st reps.

Row 1 (RS): Sl wyif, (k1, yo) three times, k1, [k3, k2tog, k2, yo, k1, yo, k2, ssk, k4] to last 6 sts, k2, (yo, k1) twice, yo, k2.

Row 2 (WS and all following WS rows): Sl wyif, k1, p to last 2 sts, k2.

Row 3: Sl wyif, (k1, yo) three times, k4, [k2, k2tog, k2, yo, k3, yo, k2, ssk, k3] to last 9 sts, k5, (yo, k1) twice, yo, k2.

Row 5: Sl wyif, (k1, yo) four times, k2, ssk, k2, [k1, k2tog, k2, yo, k5, yo, k2, ssk, k2] to last 12 sts, k1, k2tog, k2, yo, k3, (yo, k1) twice, yo, k2.

Row 7: Sl wyif, (k1, yo) three times, k5, yo, k2, ssk, k1, [k2tog, k2, yo, k7, yo, k2, ssk, k1] to last 15 sts, k2tog, k2, yo, k7, (yo, k1) twice, yo, k2.

Row 9: Sl wyif, (k1, yo) three times, k2tog, k2, yo, k1, yo, k2, ssk, k4, [k3, k2tog, k2, yo, k1, yo, k2, ssk, k4] to last 18 sts, k3, k2tog, k2, yo, k1, yo, k2, ssk, k2, (yo, k1) twice, yo, k2.

Row 11: Sl wyif, (k1, yo) three times, [k2, k2tog, k2, yo, k3, yo, k2, ssk, k3] to last 5 sts, k1, (yo, k1) twice, yo, k2.

Row 13: Sl wyif, (k1, yo) three times, k3, [k1, k2tog, k2, yo, k5, yo, k2, ssk, k2] to last 8 sts, k4, (yo, k1) twice, yo, k2.

Row 15: Sl wyif, (k1, yo) three times, k6, [k2tog, k2, yo, k7, yo, k2, ssk, k1] to last 11 sts, k7, (yo, k1) twice, yo, k2.

Row 16: Sl wyif, k1, p to last 2 sts, k2.

Row 1 (RS): Sl wyif, (k1, yo) three times, k1, [k3, k2tog, k2, yo, k1, yo, k2, ssk, k4] to last 6 sts, k2, (yo, k1) twice, yo, k2.

Row 2 (WS and all following WS rows): Sl wyif, k1, p to last 2 sts, k2.

Row 3: Sl wyif, (k1, yo) three times, k4, [k2, k2tog, k2, yo, k3, yo, k2, ssk, k3] to last 9 sts, k5, (yo, k1) twice, yo, k2.

Row 5: Sl wyif, (k1, yo) four times, k2, ssk, k2, [k1, k2tog, k2, yo, k2tog, yo, k1, yo, ssk, yo, k2, ssk, k2] to last 12 sts, k1, k2tog, k2, yo, k3, (yo, k1) twice, yo, k2.

Row 7: Sl wyif, (k1, yo) three times, k2tog, yo, k1, yo, ssk, yo, k2, ssk, k1, [k2tog, k2, (yo, k2tog) twice, yo, k1, yo, ssk, yo, k2, ssk, k1] to last 15 sts, k2tog, k2, (yo, k2tog) twice, yo, k3, (yo, k1) twice, yo, k2.

Row 9: Sl wyif, (k1, yo) three times, k2, k2tog, yo, k1 tbl, (yo, ssk) twice, yo, k2, sk2po, [k2, (yo, k2tog) twice, yo, k1 tbl, (yo, ssk) twice, yo, k2, sk2po] to last 17 sts, k2, (yo, k2tog) twice, yo, k1 tbl, yo, ssk, k4, (yo, k1) twice, yo, k2.

Row 10: Sl wyif, k1, p to last 2 sts, k2.

Key

☐ RS: knit	△ RS: sk2po
○ RS: yo	⋈ RS: k1 tbl
╲ RS: k2tog	▷ RS: slip purlwise with yarn in front
╱ RS: ssk	☐ pattern repeat

Chart A

Chart B

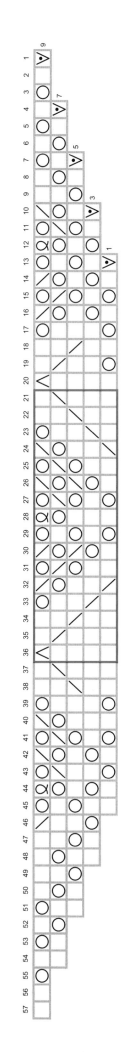
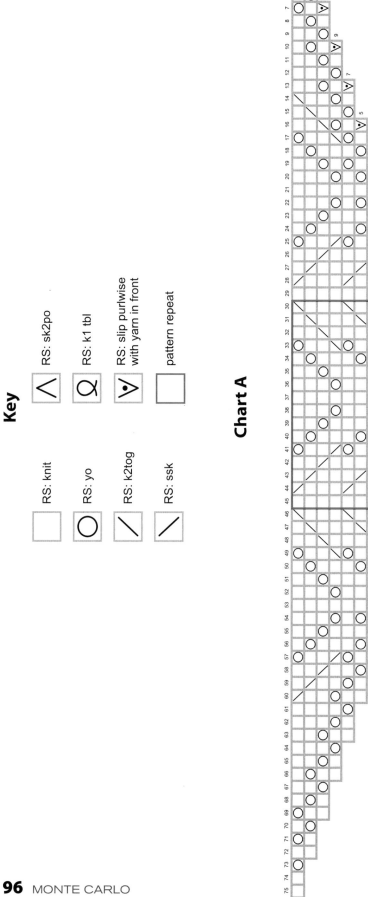

Marbella

Marbella takes full advantage of a set of gradient or self-striping mini skeins but will look just as beautiful in a solid or semisolid yarn. You could even use your stash to make up your own set of multicolor yarns.

SKILL LEVEL

Level 3

NOTES

- Marbella is worked from the bottom up and starts with a lace rectangle. Short rows are then worked in garter stitch to create the crescent shape.
- I recommend using the long-tail cast-on (also known as the thumb cast-on) holding two needles together or another very stretchy cast-on for this shawl. For a photo tutorial on the long-tail cast-on, see page 16.
- Do not use a stretchy bind-off.
- Start with C1 then change yarns throughout as you finish each mini skein (or as desired if using alternate yarn).
- Chart B shows RS rows only; see pattern for WS rows.

Finished Measurements

Wingspan: 42 in/106.5 cm
Depth: 15½ in/39.5 cm

Yarn

Sweet Georgia Tough Love Sock "Party of Five" Mini Skeins, super fine weight #1 yarn, 80% superwash merino wool/20% nylon, 105 yd/96 m, 1 oz/28 g (per mini skein), 1 set Sea to Sky, which includes

- 1 mini skein Sapphire (C1)
- 1 mini skein Salt Air (C2)
- 1 mini skein Evergreen (C3)
- 1 mini skein Fern (C4)
- 1 mini skein Basil (C5)

Needles and Other Materials

- US size 6 (4 mm) circular needle, 32 in/80 cm long
- Tapestry needle
- Stitch markers

Gauge

18 sts x 27 rows in Chart B patt after blocking = 4 in/10 cm square
Be sure to check your gauge!

Special Stitches and Techniques

Sk2po: Slip 1 stitch knitwise, knit 2 stitches together, pass slipped stitch over the k2tog stitch.

Drop yo from previous row: Pull off the next stitch from the left needle (which was a yarn over on the previous row) and allow it to drop between the needles without working it.

Insert needle under four strands and knit: Find the strands of yarn, or "ladders," between the needles; put the right needle under the strands from front to back, and knit as 1 stitch.

Multiple yarn overs: Wrap the working yarn from front to back over the working needle the designated number of yarn overs. If the next stitch is a purl stitch, take the yarn between the needles to the front ready to purl the next stitch.

Cast On

Using C1 and the long-tail cast-on holding two needles together or an alternative very stretchy cast-on method, CO 283 sts.
Row 1 (WS): K to end.
Row 2 (RS): Sl wyif, k to end.
Row 3: Sl wyif, k to end.

Work Chart A

Row 1 (RS): Work Row 1 of Chart A, working the 12-st rep 23 times.
Row 2 (WS): Work Row 2 of Chart A, working the 12-st rep 23 times.
Row 3: Work Row 3 of Chart A, working the 12-st rep 23 times.
Continue working through all 10 rows of Chart A once.

Work Chart B

Row 1 (RS): Work Row 1 of Chart B, working the 12-st rep 23 times.
Row 2 (WS and all following WS rows): Sl wyif, k2, p to last 3 sts, k3.
Row 3: Work Row 3 of Chart B, working the 12-st rep 23 times.
Continue working through all 32 rows of Chart B once, then work Rows 1–16 once more.

Work Short Rows

Row 1 (RS): Sl wyif, k to end.
Row 2 (WS): Sl wyif, k to end.
Row 3: Sl wyif, k141, ssk, k4, turn. *135 sts rem.*
Row 4: Sl wyif, k6, ssk, k4, turn. *135 sts rem.*
Each time you turn, you create a gap. If you struggle to see the gap, place a marker there.
Row 5: Sl wyif, k to 1 st before gap, ssk, k4, turn.
Row 6: Sl wyif, k to 1 st before gap, ssk, k4, turn.

Rep last 2 rows until you have 227 sts rem and all "outside" sts have been worked.

Bind off.

Finishing

Weave in all loose ends. Soak the shawl in lukewarm water. Squeeze out excess water. Stretch the shawl to size and shape and pin in place. Leave to dry. Unpin when dry.

Chart A

Pattern repeat is indicated by [ ].

Row 1 (RS): Sl wyif, k2, [k5, k2tog, yo, k5] to last 4 sts, k4.

Row 2 (WS): Sl wyif, k2, p1, [p3, p2tog tbl, drop yo from previous row, (yo) twice, p2tog, p4] to last 3 sts, k3.

Row 3: Sl wyif, k2, [k3, k2tog, drop yo from previous row, (yo) three times, ssk, k2] to last 4 sts, k4.

Row 4: Sl wyif, k2, p1, [p1, p2tog tbl, drop yo from previous row, (yo) four times, p2tog, p2] to last 3 sts, k3.

Row 5: Sl wyif, k2, [k1, k2tog, (yo) four times, drop yo from previous row, insert needle under four strands and knit, (yo) four times, ssk] to last 4 sts, k4.

Row 6: Sl wyif, k2, p1, [(p2, p1 tbl, p1, p1 tbl) twice, p2] to last 3 sts, k3.

Row 7: Sl wyif, k2, [k3, k1 tbl, k1, k1 tbl, k2, (k1 tbl, k1) twice] to last 4 sts, k4.

Row 8: Sl wyif, k2, p to last 3 sts, k3.

Row 9: Sl wyif, k to end.

Row 10: Sl wyif, k2, p to last 3 sts, k3.

Chart B

Pattern repeat is indicated by [ ].

Row 1 (RS): Sl wyif, k2, [k3, yo, ssk, yo, sk2po, yo, k2tog, yo, k2] to last 4 sts, k4.

Row 2 (WS and all following WS rows): Sl wyif, k2, p to last 3 sts, k3.

Row 3: Sl wyif, k2, [k4, yo, ssk, k1, k2tog, yo, k3] to last 4 sts, k4.

Row 5: Sl wyif, k2, [k5, yo, sk2po, yo, k4] to last 4 sts, k4.

Row 7: Sl wyif, k2, [k3, k2tog, (k1, yo) twice, k1, ssk, k2] to last 4 sts, k4.

Row 9: Sl wyif, k2, [k3, k2tog, (k1, yo) twice, k1, ssk, k2] to last 4 sts, k4.

Row 11: Sl wyif, k2, [k3, yo, ssk, k3, k2tog, yo, k2] to last 4 sts, k4.

Row 13: Sl wyif, k2, [k4, yo, ssk, k1, k2tog, yo, k3] to last 4 sts, k4.

Row 15: Sl wyif, k2, [k5, yo, sk2po, yo, k4] to last 4 sts, k4.

Row 17: Sl wyif, k2, (k2tog, yo) twice, k5, yo, ssk, yo, [sk2po, yo, k2tog, yo, k5, yo, ssk, yo] to last 5 sts, ssk, k3.

Row 19: Sl wyif, k2, [k1, k2tog, yo, k7, yo, ssk] to last 4 sts, k4.

Row 21: Sl wyif, k2, k2tog, yo, k9, yo [sk2po, yo, k9, yo] to last 5 sts, ssk, k3.

Row 23: Sl wyif, k2, [k1, yo, k1, ssk, k5, k2tog, k1, yo] to last 4 sts, k4.

Row 25: Sl wyif, k2, [k1, yo, k1, ssk, k5, k2tog, k1, yo] to last 4 sts, k4.

Row 27: Sl wyif, k2, [k2, k2tog, yo, k5, yo, ssk, k1] to last 4 sts, k4.

Row 29: Sl wyif, k2, [k1, k2tog, yo, k7, yo, ssk] to last 4 sts, k4.

Row 31: Sl wyif, k2, k2tog, yo, k9, yo, [sk2po, yo, k9, yo] to last 5 sts, ssk, k3.

Row 32: Sl wyif, k2, p to last 3 sts, k3.

Chart A

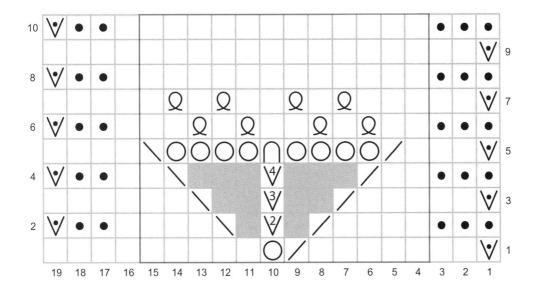

Chart Notes: Only RS rows are charted. Each chart has its own chart key.

Key A

☐	RS: knit WS: purl
╱	RS: k2tog WS: p2tog
╲	RS: ssk WS: p2tog tbl
∩	RS: drop yo from previous row, insert needle under 4 strands & knit
V2/	WS: drop yo from previous row & yo twice
V3/	RS: drop yo from previous row & yo three times
V4/	WS: drop yo from previous row & yo four times
○	RS: yo
Ω	RS: k1 tbl WS: p1 tbl
V·	RS/WS: slip purlwise with yarn in front
●	WS: knit
☐	pattern repeat
▨	no stitch

Chart B

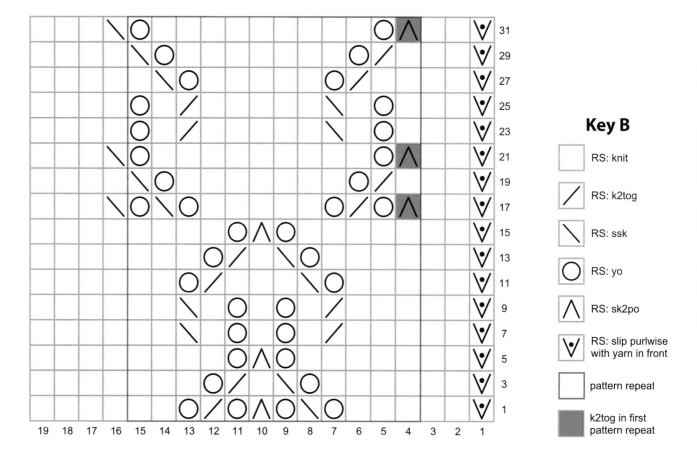

Key B

☐	RS: knit
╱	RS: k2tog
╲	RS: ssk
◯	RS: yo
⋀	RS: sk2po
⩔	RS: slip purlwise with yarn in front
☐	pattern repeat
■	k2tog in first pattern repeat

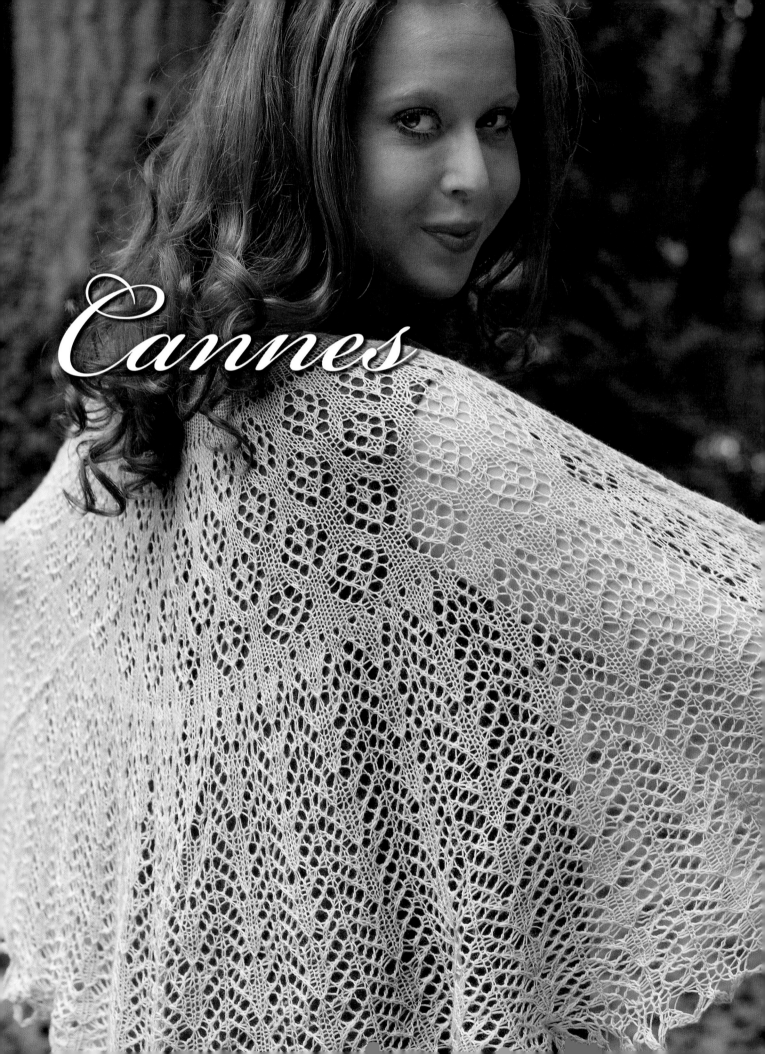

Cannes

Cannes is a stunning, glamorous shawl that is light as air. Worked in a delicate pure merino yarn, this shawl is the perfect accessory.

SKILL LEVEL

Level 3

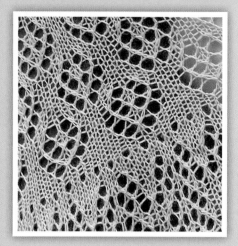

NOTES

- This shawl is worked from the center outward in a semicircle with a knitted-on edging.
- Charts A and B show RS rows only; see pattern for WS rows.
- See photo tutorials on how to work the cable cast-on on page 12, the Russian bind-off on page 17, and sewn bind-off on page 19.

Finished Measurements

Wingspan: 60 in/152.5 cm
Depth: 27½ in/70 cm

Yarn

Manos del Uruguay Marina, lace weight #0 yarn, 100% superwash merino wool, 874 yd/800 m, 3.5 oz/100 g
- 1 skein #N0036 Lavanda

Needles and Other Materials

- US size 4 (3.5 mm) needles (32 in/80 cm circular needle is recommended)
- US size 5 (3.75 mm) needles
- Tapestry needle

Gauge

26 sts x 23 rows in Chart A patt using size 5 (3.75 mm) needles after blocking = 4 in/10 cm square
Be sure to check your gauge!

Special Stitches and Techniques

Sk2po: Slip 1 stitch knitwise, knit 2 stitches together, pass the slipped stitch over the k2tog stitch.

Single join (SJ): Join 1 stitch from the edging with 1 stitch from the main shawl by knitting together the last edging stitch with 1 stitch from the main shawl.

Cable cast-on (CCO): Insert the right needle between the first 2 sts on the left needle; wrap yarn as if to knit and pull through a loop. Transfer this stitch to the left needle—3 sts on the left. Insert the right needle between the first two sts as before and make a knit st on the right needle that you transfer to the left. Continue until you have the desired number of sts.

Russian bind-off: Knit 2 stitches. *Insert the left needle into the front of those 2 stitches and knit both stitches together (or slip both stitches back to the left needle and knit them through the back loop). This leaves 1 stitch on the right needle. Knit 1. Repeat from * until the correct number of stitches have been bound off. Once you've bound off the required stitches, you will be left with 1 stitch on your right needle. Break the yarn and pull it through this stitch as for a normal bind-off.

Begin Shawl

Using size 4 (3.5 mm) needles, CO 6 sts. Knit 1 row.

Row 1 (RS): Sl wyif, k1, (yo, k1) twice, yo, k2. *3 sts inc.; 9 sts.*

Row 2 (WS and all following WS rows): Sl wyif, k2, p to last 3 sts, k3.

Row 3: Sl wyif, k1, (yo, k1) 5 times, yo, k2. *6 sts inc.; 15 sts.*

Rows 5 and 7: Sl wyif, k to end.

Row 9: Sl wyif, k1, (yo, k1) 11 times, yo, k2. *12 sts inc.; 27 sts.*

Rows 11 and 13: Sl wyif, k to end.

Row 15: Sl wyif, k1, (yo, k1) 23 times, yo, k2. *24 sts inc.; 51 sts.*

Rows 17, 19, 21, and 23: Sl wyif, k to end.

Row 25: Sl wyif, k1, (yo, k1) to last 2 sts, yo, k2. *48 sts inc.; 99 sts.*

Rows 27, 29, 31, 33, 35, 37, 39, and 41: Sl wyif, k to end.

Row 43: Sl wyif, k1, (yo, k1) to last 2 sts, yo, k2. *195 sts.*

Row 45: Sl wyif, k to end.

Row 46: Sl wyif, k2, p to last 3 sts, k3.

Work Chart A

Change to size 5 (3.75mm) needles.

Row 1 (RS): Work Row 1 of Chart A, working the 10-st rep 19 times.

Row 2 (WS and all following WS rows): Sl wyif, k2, p to last 3 sts, k3.

Row 3: Work Row 3 of Chart A, working the 10-st rep 19 times.

Continue as established, working through all 20 rows of Chart A twice.

Single Join: Knitted-On Edging

Single joins are used to attach an edging to a live stitch.

1. Knit to the last stitch of the edging (blue yarn in photos).

2. Knit last edging stitch and one live stitch together (can be worked as a k2tog, k2tog tbl, or ssk).

Transition

Row 1 (RS): Sl wyif, k to end.
Row 2 (WS): Sl wyif, k2, p to last 3 sts, k3.
Row 3: Sl wyif, k1, (yo, k2) to last 3 sts, yo, k3. *291 sts.*
Row 4: Sl wyif, k2, p to last 3 sts, k3.
Row 5: Sl wyif, k to end.
Row 6: Sl wyif, k2, p to last 3 sts, k3.

Work Chart B

Row 1 (RS): Work Row 1 of Chart B, working the 10-st rep 28 times.
Row 2 (WS and all following WS rows): Sl wyif, k2, p to last 3 sts, k3.
Row 3: Work Row 3 of Chart B, working the 10-st rep 28 times.
Continue as established, working through all 12 rows of Chart B a total of eight times. *291 sts.*

Do not break yarn.

Edging

CO 5 sts in front of the live sts using the cable cast-on.

Setup Rows

Row 1 (RS): K4, SJ, turn.
Row 2 (WS): Sl wyif, k4.
Row 3: Sl wyif, k3, SJ, turn.
Row 4: Sl wyif, k4.

Work Chart C

Row 1 (RS): Work Row 1 of Chart C, turn.
Row 2 (WS): Work Row 2 of Chart C.
Row 3: Work Row 3 of Chart C, turn.
Continue working through all 8 rows of Chart C a total
  of 72 times.

Row 1 (RS): Sl wyif, k3, SJ, turn.
Row 2 (WS): Sl wyif, k4.

Bind off using the Russian bind-off.

Finishing

Weave in all loose ends. Soak the shawl in lukewarm
  water. Squeeze out excess water. Stretch the shawl
  to size and shape and pin in place. Leave to dry.
  Unpin when dry.

Chart A

Pattern repeat is indicated by [ ].
Row 1 (RS): Sl wyif, k1, [k3, k2tog, yo, k1, yo, ssk, k2] to
  last 3 sts, k3.
Row 2 (WS and all following WS rows): Sl wyif, k2, p to
  last 3 sts, k3.
Row 3: Sl wyif, k1, [k2, k2tog, yo, k3, yo, ssk, k1] to last 3
  sts, k3.
Row 5: Sl wyif, k1, [k2, yo, ssk, yo, sk2po, yo, k2tog, yo,
  k1] to last 3 sts, k3.
Row 7: Sl wyif, k1, [k3, yo, ssk, k1, k2tog, yo, k2] to last 3
  sts, k3.
Row 9: Sl wyif, k1, [k4, yo, sk2po, yo, k3] to last 3 sts, k3.
Row 11: Sl wyif, k1, [k1, yo, ssk, k5, k2tog, yo] to last 3
  sts, k3.
Row 13: Sl wyif, k1, [k2, yo, ssk, k3, k2tog, yo, k1] to last
  3 sts, k3.

Row 15: Sl wyif, k1, (k2tog, yo) twice, yo, k3, yo, ssk, yo
  [sk2po, yo, k2tog, yo, k3, yo, ssk, yo] to last 4 sts, ssk,
  k2.
Row 17: Sl wyif, k1, [k1, k2tog, yo, k5, yo, ssk] to last 3
  sts, k3.
Row 19: Sl wyif, k1, k2tog, yo, k7, yo, [sk2po, yo, k7, yo]
  to last 4 sts, ssk, k2.
Row 20: Sl wyif, k2, p to last 3 sts, k3.

Chart B

Pattern repeat is indicated by [ ].
Row 1 (RS): Sl wyif, k1, yo, ssk, k1, [k2, k2tog, yo, k3, yo,
  ssk, k1] to last 6 sts, k2, k2tog, yo, k2.
Row 2 (WS and all following WS rows): Sl wyif, k2, p to
  last 3 sts, k3.

Row 3: Sl wyif, k2, yo, ssk, [k1, (k2tog, yo) twice, k1, (yo, ssk) twice] to last 6 sts, k1, k2tog, yo, k3.

Row 5: Sl wyif, k4, [k2, k2tog, yo, k3, yo, ssk, k1] to last 6 sts, k6.

Row 7: Sl wyif, k3, yo, [sk2po, yo, k1, k2tog, yo, k1, yo, ssk, k1, yo] to last 7 sts, sk2po, yo, k4.

Row 9: Sl wyif, k1, yo, ssk, k1, [k2, k2tog, yo, k3, yo, ssk, k1] to last 6 sts, k2, k2tog, yo, k2.

Row 11: Sl wyif, k2, yo, ssk, [k1, (k2tog, yo) twice, k1, (yo, ssk) twice] to last 6 sts, k1, k2tog, yo, k3.

Row 12: Sl wyif, k2, p to last 3 sts, k3.

Chart C

Row 1 (RS): Sl wyif, k3, SJ.

Row 2 (WS): Sl wyif, k4.

Row 3: Sl wyif, k3, SJ.

Row 4: Sl wyif, k1, (yo) three times, k3.

Row 5: Sl wyif, k2, (k1 tbl, k1) twice, SJ.

Row 6: Sl wyif, k2, k1 tbl, k4.

Row 7: RBO3, k3, SJ.

Row 8: Sl wyif, k4.

Chart A

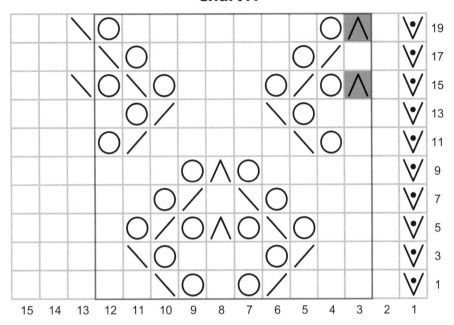

Chart B

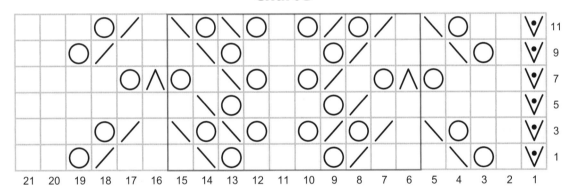

Key

☐	RS: knit / WS: purl
ⱽ	RS/WS: slip purlwise with yarn in front
○	RS/WS: yo
╱	RS: k2tog
✕	stitch left from RBO
•	WS: knit
Ω	RS/WS: k1 tbl
∧	RS: sk2po
ⱽ̲	RS: SJ
∩	RBO
╲	RS: ssk
☐	pattern repeat
▨	work as k2tog in first rep

Chart C

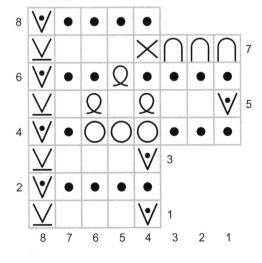

St. Tropez

St. Tropez has a simple triangle shape with an allover beautiful lace pattern. Elegant and light as a feather, this shawl can be worn wrapped around your neck as a scarf or to keep your shoulders warm on a cool summer night.

Finished Measurements

Width: 75 in/190.5 cm
Depth: 31½ in/80 cm

Yarn

The Yarn Collective Portland Lace, lace weight #0 yarn, 100% merino wool, 940 yd/860 m, 3.5 oz/100 g
- 1 skein #210 Daydreaming

Needles and Other Materials

- US size 4 (3.5 mm) circular needle, 32 in/80 cm long
- Tapestry needle
- 2 locking stitch markers (optional)

Gauge

19 sts x 26½ rows in Chart D patt after blocking = 4 in/10 cm square
Be sure to check your gauge!

Special Stitches and Techniques

Sk2po: Slip 1 stitch knitwise, knit 2 stitches together, pass slipped stitch over the k2tog stitch.

Russian bind-off: Knit 2 stitches. *Insert the left needle into the front of those 2 stitches and knit both stitches together (or slip both stitches back to the left needle and knit through the back loop). This leaves 1 stitch on the right needle. Knit 1. Repeat from * until the correct number of stitches have been bound off. Once you've bound off the required stitches, you will be left with 1 stitch on your right needle. Break the yarn and pull it through this stitch as for a normal bind-off.

SKILL LEVEL

Level 3

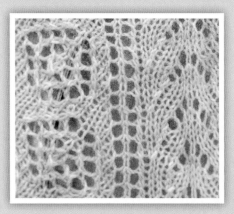

NOTES

- You may wish to put a locking stitch marker on the stitches in bold. These markers indicate the "spines." You will increase either side of both spines as well as inside the first 2 and last 2 stitches for the first 16 rows. After that you will continue to increase 4 stitches every right-side row: after the first 2 stitches, before the first spine, after the second spine, and before the last 2 stitches. Placing locking stitch markers on the spine stitches will help you remember to increase as directed and keep your place in the pattern.
- See page 17 for a photo tutorial on the Russian bind-off.
- Charts show RS rows only; see pattern for WS rows.

Work Charts A and B

CO 9 sts. Knit 1 row.

Row 1 (RS): K2, work Row 1 of Chart A, **k1**, work Row 1 of Chart B, **k1**, work Row 1 of Chart A, k2. *6 sts inc.*

Row 2 (WS and all following WS rows): K2, p to last 2 sts, k2.

Row 3: K2, work Row 3 of Chart A, **k1**, work Row 3 of Chart B, **k1**, work Row 3 of Chart A, k2. *6 sts inc.*

Continue working through all 16 rows of Charts A and B. *57 sts.*

Work Charts C and D

Row 1: K2, work Row 1 of Chart C, working the 12-st rep once, **k1**, work Row 1 of Chart D once, **k1**, work Row 1 of Chart C, working the 12-st rep once, k2. *4 sts inc.*

Row 2 (WS and all following WS rows): K2, p to last 2 sts, k2.

Row 3: K2, work Row 3 of Chart C, working the 12-st rep once, **k1**, work Row 3 of Chart D once, **k1**, work Row 3 of Chart C, working the 12-st rep once, k2. *4 sts inc.*

Continue working through all 12 rows of Charts C and D 15 times. For each subsequent 12-row rep of Charts C and D, work an additional 12-st rep of Chart C in each section. *417 sts.*

Work Charts E and F

Row 1: K2, work Row 1 of Chart E, working the 12-st rep 16 times, **k1**, work Row 1 of Chart F once, **k1**, work Row 1 of Chart E, working the 12-st rep 16 times, k2. *4 sts inc.*

Row 2 (WS and all following WS rows): K2, p to last 2 sts, k2.

Row 3: K2, work Row 3 of Chart E, working the 12-st rep 16 times, **k1**, work Row 3 of Chart F once, **k1**, work Row 3 of Chart E, working the 12-st rep 16 times, k2. *4 sts inc.*

Continue working through all 14 rows of Charts E and F once. *445 sts.*

Bind off using the Russian bind-off.

Finishing

Weave in all loose ends. Soak the shawl in lukewarm water. Squeeze out excess water. Stretch the shawl to size and shape and pin in place. Leave to dry. Unpin when dry.

Chart A

Row 1 (RS): Yo, k1, yo.
Row 2 (WS and all following WS rows): See pattern.
Row 3: Yo, k3, yo.
Row 5: Yo, k5, yo.
Row 7: Yo, k7, yo.
Row 9: Yo, k2, k2tog, yo, k1, yo, ssk, k2, yo.
Row 11: Yo, k2, k2tog, yo, k3, yo, ssk, k2, yo.
Row 13: Yo, k2, (k2tog, yo) twice, k1, (yo, ssk) twice, k2, yo.

Row 15: Yo, k2, (k2tog, yo) twice, k3, (yo, ssk) twice, k2, yo.
Row 16: See pattern.

Chart B

Row 1 (RS): Yo, k1, yo.
Row 2 (WS and all following WS rows): See pattern.
Row 3: Yo, k3, yo.
Row 5: Yo, k5, yo.
Row 7: Yo, k7, yo.
Row 9: Yo, k9, yo.
Row 11: Yo, k1, k2tog, k2, yo, k1, yo, k2, ssk, k1, yo.
Row 13: Yo, k1, k2tog, k2, yo, k3, yo, k2, ssk, k1, yo.
Row 15: Yo, k1, k2tog, k2, yo, k5, yo, k2, ssk, k1, yo.
Row 16: See pattern.

Chart A

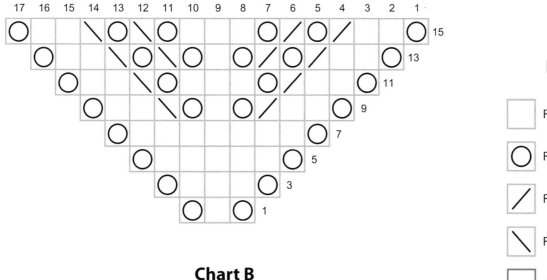

Key

- □ RS: knit
- ○ RS: yo
- ╱ RS: k2tog
- ╲ RS: ssk
- □ pattern repeat

Chart B

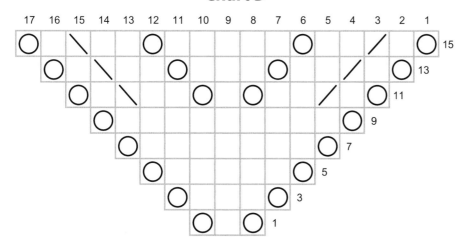

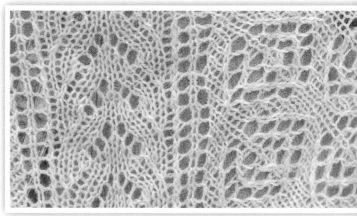

Chart D

Row 1 (RS): Yo, ssk, k2, k2tog, k2, yo, k1, yo, k2, ssk, k2, k2tog, yo.
Row 2 (WS and all following WS rows): See pattern.
Row 3: Yo, ssk, k1, k2tog, k2, yo, k3, yo, k2, ssk, k1, k2tog, yo.
Row 5: Yo, ssk, k2tog, k2, yo, k5, yo, k2, ssk, k2tog, yo.
Row 7: Yo, ssk, k2, k2tog, k2, yo, k1, yo, k2, ssk, k2, k2tog, yo.
Row 9: Yo, ssk, k1, k2tog, k2, yo, k3, yo, k2, ssk, k1, k2tog, yo.
Row 11: Yo, ssk, k2tog, k2, yo, k5, yo, k2, ssk, k2tog, yo.
Row 12: See pattern.

Chart E

Pattern repeat is in [ ].
Row 1 (RS): Yo, k2, [k1, ssk, k3, yo, k1, yo, k3, k2tog] 16 times, k3, yo.
Row 2 (WS and all following WS rows): See pattern.
Row 3: Yo, k3, [k1, ssk, k2, yo, k3, yo, k2, k2tog] 16 times, k4, yo.
Row 5: Yo, k2, k2tog, yo, [(k1, yo, ssk) twice, (k1, k2tog, yo) twice] 16 times, k1, yo, ssk, k2, yo.
Row 7: Yo, k2, k2tog, yo, k1, [k2, yo, ssk, k1, yo, sk2po, yo, k1, k2tog, yo, k1] 16 times, k2, yo, ssk, k2, yo.
Row 9: Yo, k2, (k2tog, yo) twice, [k1, (yo, ssk) twice, k3, (k2tog, yo) twice] 16 times, k1, (yo, ssk) twice, k2, yo.
Row 11: Yo, k2, (k2tog, yo) twice, k1, [k2, (yo, ssk) twice, k1, (k2tog, yo) twice, k1] 16 times, k2, (yo, ssk) twice, k2, yo.
Row 13: Yo, k2, (k2tog, yo) three times, [k1, (yo, ssk) twice, yo, sk2po, (yo, k2tog) twice, yo] 16 times, k1, (yo, ssk) three times, k2, yo.
Row 14: See pattern.

Chart C

Pattern repeat is in [ ].
For each subsequent 12-row rep, work an additional 12-st rep in each section.
Row 1 (RS): Yo, k2, [k3, yo, ssk, yo, sk2po, yo, k2tog, yo, k2] once, k3, yo.
Row 2 (WS and all following WS rows): See pattern.
Row 3: Yo, k3, [k4, yo, ssk, k1, k2tog, yo, k3] once, k4, yo.
Row 5: Yo, k2, k2tog, yo, [k1, yo, ssk, k2, yo, sk2po, yo, k2, k2tog, yo] once, k1, yo, ssk, k2, yo.
Row 7: Yo, k2, k2tog, yo, k1, [k2, yo, ssk, k5, k2tog, yo, k1] once, k2, yo, ssk, k2, yo.
Row 9: Yo, k2, (k2tog, yo) twice, [k1, (yo, ssk) twice, k3, (k2tog, yo) twice] once, k1, (yo, ssk) twice, k2, yo.
Row 11: Yo, k2, (k2tog, yo) twice, k1, [k2, (yo, ssk) twice, k1, (k2tog, yo) twice, k1] once, k2, (yo, ssk) twice, k2, yo.
Row 12: See pattern.

Chart C

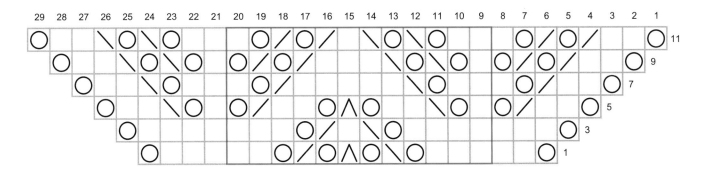

Chart D

Key

☐	RS: knit
○	RS: yo
╱	RS: k2tog
╲	RS: ssk
☐	pattern repeat

Chart E

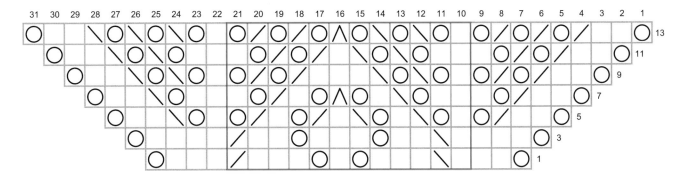

Chart F

Row 1 (RS): Yo, ssk, k2, k2tog, k2, yo, k1, yo, k2, ssk, k2, k2tog, yo.

Row 2 (WS and all following WS rows): See pattern.

Row 3: Yo, ssk, k1, k2tog, k2, yo, k3, yo, k2, ssk, k1, k2tog, yo.

Row 5: Yo, ssk, k2tog, k2, yo, k5, yo, k2, ssk, k2tog, yo.

Row 7: Yo, ssk, k2, (k2tog, yo) twice, k1, (yo, ssk) twice, k2, k2tog, yo.

Row 9: Yo, ssk, k1, (k2tog, yo) twice, k3, (yo, ssk) twice, k1, k2tog, yo.

Row 11: Yo, ssk, (k2tog, yo) twice, k5, (yo, ssk) twice, k2tog, yo.

Row 13: Yo, sk2po, yo, (k2tog, yo, k1) twice, yo, ssk, k1, yo, ssk, yo, sk2po, yo.

Row 14: See pattern.

Key

- ☐ RS: knit
- ◯ RS: yo
- ╱ RS: k2tog
- ╲ RS: ssk
- ☐ pattern repeat

Chart F

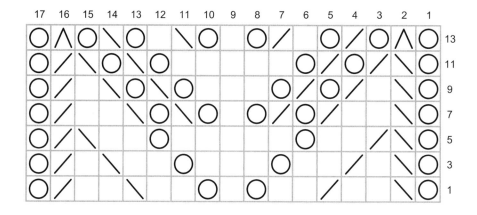

Barcelona

Barcelona is a stunning stole adorned with beads to create a real showstopper. It is perfect to wear over a little black dress or as a glamorous scarf.

SKILL LEVEL

Level 3

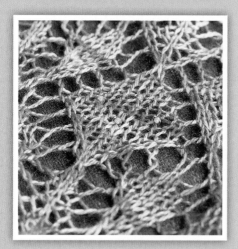

NOTES

- Beads are added using the crochet hook method. See page 22 for a photo tutorial.
- See page 17 for a photo tutorial on how to work the Russian bind-off.

Finished Measurements

Width: 20 in/51 cm
Length: 82 in/208 cm

Yarn

Fyberspates Gleem Lace, lace weight #0 yarn, 55% Bluefaced Leicester wool/45% silk, 874 yd/800 m, 3.5 oz/100 g

- 1 skein #711 Mixed Magentas

Needles and Other Materials

- US size 4 (3.5 mm) straight needles
- 141 size 6 seed beads (shown in Debbie Abrahams color #207)
- US size 15 (0.5 mm) steel crochet hook
- Tapestry needle

Gauge

16 sts x 28 rows in Chart patt after blocking = 4 in/10 cm square
Be sure to check your gauge!

Special Stitches and Techniques

Add beads using the crochet hook method (B): Place a bead on the crochet hook, lift st off left needle using the crochet hook and slip the bead onto the st. Replace the st on left needle and knit.

Sk2po: Slip 1 stitch knitwise, knit 2 stitches together, pass the slipped stitch over the k2tog stitch.

Russian bind-off (RBO): Knit 2 stitches. *Insert the left needle into the front of those 2 stitches and knit both stitches together (or slip both stitches back to the left needle and knit through back loop). This leaves 1 stitch on the right needle. Knit 1. Repeat from * until the correct number of stitches have been bound off. Once you've bound off the required stitches, you will be left with 1 stitch on your right needle. Break the yarn and pull it through this stitch as for a normal bind-off.

Begin Shawl

CO 78 sts.
Row 1 (RS): Sl wyif, k to end.
Row 2 (WS): Sl wyif, k to end.
Rep the last 2 rows two more times (6 rows of garter st worked).

Work Chart

Row 1 (RS): Work Row 1 of Chart, working the 18-st rep three times. *1 st inc.*
Row 2 (WS): Work Row 2 of Chart, working the 18-st rep three times. *1 st inc.*
Row 3: Work Row 3 of Chart, working the 18-st rep three times.
Row 4: Work Row 4 of Chart, working the 18-st rep three times.
Continue working through all 28 rows of Chart a total of 20 times.

Work Garter Stitch Edge

Row 1 (RS): Sl wyif, k to end.
Row 2 (WS): Sl wyif, k to end.

Rep last 2 rows two more times (6 rows of garter st worked).
Bind off using the Russian bind-off.

Finishing

Weave in all loose ends. Soak the shawl in lukewarm water. Squeeze out excess water. Stretch the shawl to size and shape and pin in place. Leave to dry. Unpin when dry.

Chart

Pattern repeat is indicated by [ ].
Row 1 (RS): Sl wyif, k3, k2tog, yo, ssk, k4, yo, k1, [k2, yo, k4, k2tog, yo, sk2po, yo, ssk, k4, yo, k1] three times, k1, k2tog, yo, k1, ssk, k2, yo, k1, m1, k2.
Row 2 (WS): Sl wyif, k1, p6, k2tog, yo, k1, p to last 4 sts, k4.
Row 3: Sl wyif, k5, yo, sk2po, k2, yo, k2, [k3, yo, k2, sk2po, yo, k3, yo, sk2po, k2, yo, k2] three times, k1, k2tog, yo, k1, ssk, k1, yo, k5.
Row 4: Repeat Row 2.
Row 5: Sl wyif, k5, yo, sk2po, k1, yo, k3, [B, k3, yo, k1, k2tog, yo, k1, sk2po, k1, yo, ssk, k1, yo, k3] three times, k1, k2tog, yo, k1, ssk, yo, k4, m1, k2.

Row 6: Sl wyif, k1, p7, k2tog, yo, k1, p to last 4 sts, k4.

Row 7: Sl wyif, k5, yo, sk2po, yo, k2, B, k1, [k2, B, k2, yo, k2tog, yo, k1, sk2po, k1, yo, ssk, yo, k4] three times, k1, k2tog, yo, k1, ssk, k3, yo, k4.

Row 8: Repeat Row 6.

Row 9: Sl wyif, k5, k2tog, yo, k1, yo, ssk, k2, [B, k2, k2tog, yo, k1, yo, k2, sk2po, k2, yo, k1, yo, ssk, k2] three times, k1, k2tog, yo, k1, ssk, k2, yo, k3, m1, k2.

Row 10: Sl wyif, k1, p8, k2tog, yo, k1, p to last 4 sts, k4.

Row 11: Sl wyif, k4, k2tog, yo, k3, yo, ssk, k1, [k2, k2tog, yo, k3, yo, k1, sk2po, k1, yo, k3, yo, ssk, k1] three times, k1, k2tog, yo, k1, ssk, k1, yo, k7.

Row 12: Repeat Row 10.

Row 13: Sl wyif, k3, k2tog, yo, k5, yo, ssk, [k1, k2tog, yo, k5, yo, sk2po, yo, k5, yo, ssk] three times, k1, k2tog, yo, k1, ssk, yo, k6, m1, k2.

Row 14: RBO4, k1, p5, k2tog, yo, k1, p to last 4 sts, k4.

Row 15: Sl wyif, k5, yo, k4, k2tog, yo, [sk2po, yo, ssk, k4, yo, k3, yo, k4, k2tog, yo] three times, ssk, k2tog, yo, k1, ssk, k2, yo, k1, m1, k2.

Row 16: Repeat Row 2.

Row 17: Sl wyif, k6, yo, k2, sk2po, yo, k1, [k2, yo, sk2po, k2, yo, k5, yo, k2, sk2po, yo, k1] three times, k1, k2tog, yo, k1, ssk, k1, yo, k5.

Row 18: Repeat Row 2.

Row 19: Sl wyif, k7, yo, k1, k2tog, yo, k1, [sk2po, k1, yo, ssk, k1, yo, k3, B, k3, yo, k1, k2tog, yo, k1] three times, ssk, k2tog, yo, k1, ssk, yo, k4, m1, k2.

Row 20: Repeat Row 6.

Row 21: Sl wyif, k8, yo, k2tog, yo, k1, [sk2po, k1, yo, ssk, yo, k2, B, k3, B, k2, yo, k2tog, yo, k1] three times, ssk, k2tog, yo, k1, ssk, k3, yo, k4.

Row 22: Repeat Row 6.

Row 23: Sl wyif, k6, k2tog, yo, k1, yo, k2, [sk2po, k2, yo, k1, yo, ssk, k2, B, k2, k2tog, yo, k1, yo, k2] three times, ssk, k2tog, yo, k1, ssk, k2, yo, k3, m1, k2.

Row 24: Repeat Row 10.

Row 25: Sl wyif, k5, k2tog, yo, k3, yo, k1, [sk2po, k1, yo, k3, yo, ssk, k3, k2tog, yo, k3, yo, k1] three times, ssk, k2tog, yo, k1, ssk, k1, yo, k7.

Row 26: Repeat Row 10.

Row 27: Sl wyif, k4, k2tog, yo, k5, yo, [sk2po, yo, k5, yo, ssk, k1, k2tog, yo, k5, yo] three times, ssk, k2tog, yo, k1, ssk, yo, k6, m1, k2.

Row 28: RBO4, k1, p5, k2tog, yo, k1, p to last 4 sts, k4.

Key

Chart

RS: knit
WS: purl

RS: yo ○

RS/WS: k2tog /

RS: ssk \

RS: sk2po ∧

add bead and knit B

RBO ∪

stitch left from RBO ✕

RS: m1 ♌

RS/WS: slip purlwise with yarn in front ⋗

WS: knit ●

pattern repeat □

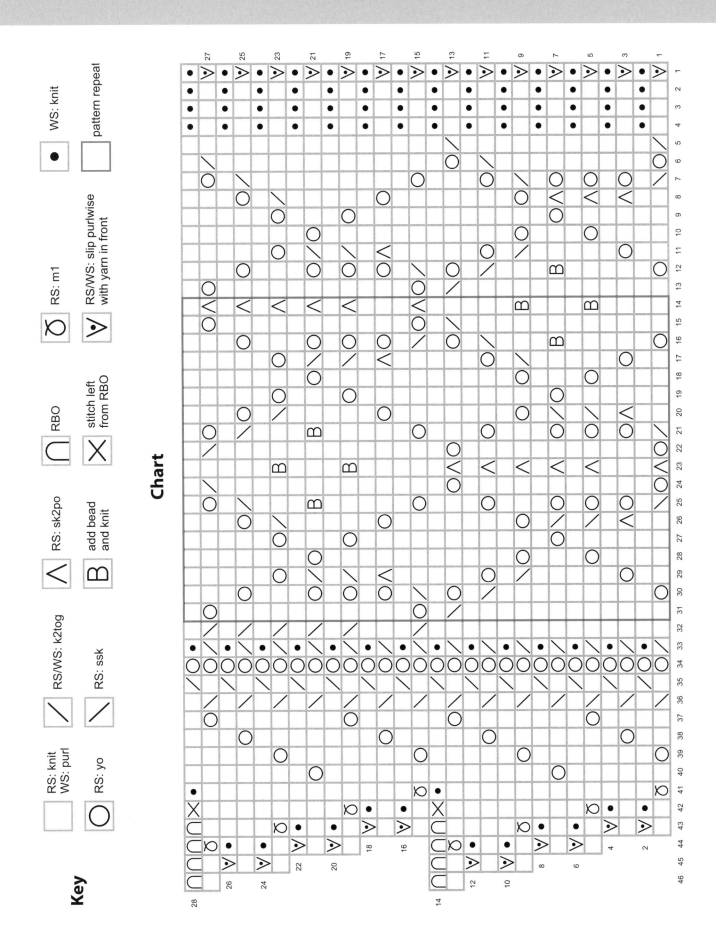

Larnaca

Two rectangles are transformed into a light-as-air poncho perfect to wear for a bit of warmth without the weight of a heavy garment. The alpaca yarn is fine but still warm.

Finished Measurements

Sizes: Small (Medium, Large)
Width: 28 (32$\frac{1}{4}$, 35$\frac{1}{2}$) in/71 (82, 90) cm
Length: 21 (23$\frac{1}{2}$, 25$\frac{3}{4}$) in/53.5 (59.5, 65.5) cm
This piece is knitted sideways so the rows run up and down. You can customize your size by casting on more stitches in groups of 12 for a longer poncho and/or working more 12-row repeats for a wider poncho.

Yarn

Cascade Alpaca Lace, lace weight #0 yarn, 100% baby alpaca, 437 yd/ 400 m, 1.75 oz/50 g
- 3 (4, 5) skeins #1440 Antique Moss

Needles and Other Materials

- US size 4 (3.5 mm) needles
- Stitch markers

Gauge

20 sts x 28 rows in Chart patt after blocking = 4 in/10 cm square
Be sure to check your gauge!

Special Stitches and Techniques

Russian bind-off: Knit 2 stitches. *Insert the left needle into the front of those 2 stitches and knit both stitches together (or slip both stitches back to the left needle and knit through back loop). This leaves 1 stitch on the right needle. Knit 1. Repeat from * until the correct number of stitches have been bound off. Once you've bound off the required stitches, you will be left with 1 stitch on your right needle. Break the yarn and pull it through this stitch as for a normal bind-off.

SKILL LEVEL

Level 3

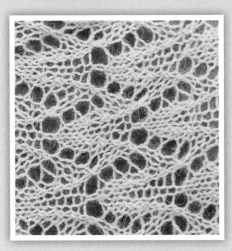

NOTES

- When checking measurements during knitting, stretch the piece to simulate blocking.
- The poncho is worked sideways in two pieces. The top edge is seamed, leaving a gap in the center to fit over your head. You can also seam the sides, although they can be left open if preferred.
- See page 17 for a photo tutorial on how to work the Russian bind-off.
- Charts show RS rows only; see pattern for WS rows.

Begin Garter Stitch Section

CO 105 (117, 129) sts using a stretchy cast-on.
Row 1 (WS): K to end.
Row 2 (RS): Sl wyif, k to end.
Rep last row three more times (5 rows worked in total).

Work Chart

Row 1 (RS): Work Row 1 of Chart, working the 12-st rep 8 (9, 10) times.
Row 2 (WS and all following WS rows): Sl wyif, k3, p to last 4 sts, k4.
Row 3: Work Row 3 of Chart, working the 12-st rep 8 (9, 10) times.
Continue working through all 12 rows of Chart 16 (18, 20) times.

Work Garter Stitch

Row 1 (RS): Sl wyif, k to end.
Rep Row 1 four more times (5 rows worked).
Bind off using the Russian bind-off.

Finishing

Weave in all loose ends. Soak both pieces in lukewarm water. Squeeze out excess water. Stretch both rectangles to size and shape and pin in place. Leave to dry. Unpin when dry.

Seam the top edge together (along the rows), leaving a gap measuring approximately 8 in/20.5 cm in the center to fit over the head. Seam approximately 2 in/5 cm at the bottom of the sides (along the cast-on or bind-off edge).

Chart

Pattern repeat is in [ ].

Row 1 (RS): Sl wyif, k3, [k1, ssk, k1, yo, k2tog, yo, k1, yo, ssk, yo, k1, k2tog] to last 5 sts, k5.

Row 2 (WS and all following WS rows): Sl wyif, k3, p to last 4 sts, k4.

Row 3: Sl wyif, k3, [k1, ssk, k2, yo, k3, yo, k2, k2tog] to last 5 sts, k5.

Row 5: Sl wyif, k3, [k1, ssk, k1, yo, k5, yo, k1, k2tog] to last 5 sts, k5.

Row 7: Sl wyif, k3, [k1, yo, ssk, yo, k1, k2tog, k1, ssk, k1, yo, k2tog, yo] to last 5 sts, k5.

Row 9: Sl wyif, k3, [k2, yo, k2, k2tog, k1, ssk, k2, yo, k1] to last 5 sts, k5.

Row 11: Sl wyif, k3, [k3, yo, k1, k2tog, k1, ssk, k1, yo, k2] to last 5 sts, k5.

Row 12: Sl wyif, k3, p to last 4 sts, k4.

Key

☐	RS: knit
V̇	RS: slip purlwise with yarn in front
○	RS: yo
/	RS: k2tog
\	RS: ssk
☐	pattern repeat

Chart

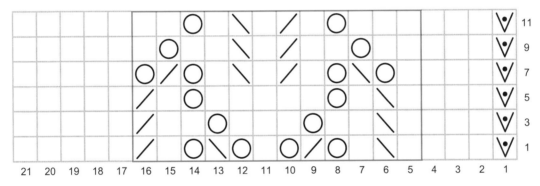

21 20 19 18 17 16 15 14 13 12 11 10 9 8 7 6 5 4 3 2 1

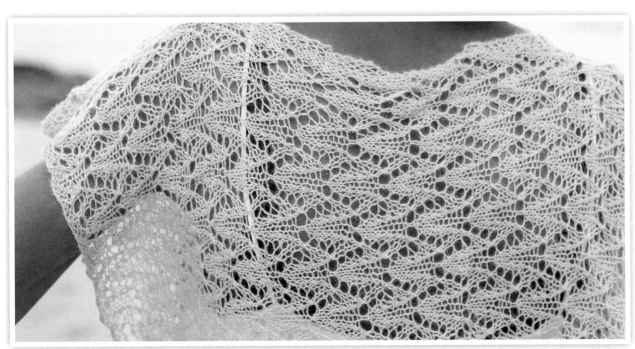

Abbreviations

B	bead	rep	repeat
beg	beginning	rnd(s)	round(s)
CCO	cable cast-on	RS	right side
CO	cast on	s2kpo	slip 2 stitches knitwise, knit 1 stitch, pass slipped stitches over
dec	decrease(d)		
inc	increase(d)	SJ	single join
k	knit	sk2po	slip 1 stitch knitwise, k2tog, pass slipped stitch over
k2tog	knit 2 sts together		
kfbf	knit into front, back, then front of the same stitch	sl	slip
		sl wyib	slip stitch purlwise with yarn in back
m	marker		
m1	lift the strand between two needles and knit through the back loop	sl wyif	slip stitch purlwise with yarn in front, then take the yarn between the stitches to the back
p	purl	sm	slip marker
p2tog	purl 2 sts together	ssk	slip one stitch knitwise, slip another stitch knitwise, insert left needle into the front of both stitches and knit tog
p2tog tbl	insert right needle in back of 2nd st on left needle, then in back of 1st st; loop yarn around right needle as if to purl and pull through a loop; slip sts off left needle		
		st(s)	stitch(es)
		St st	stockinette stitch
patt	pattern	tbl	through back loop
pm	place marker	tog	together
psso	pass slipped stitch over	WS	wrong side
RBO	Russian bind-off	yo	yarn over

Yarn Sources

Berroco
berroco.com

Cascade
cascadeyarns.com

Debbie Bliss
debbieblissonline.com

Drops Design
garnstudio.com

Freia Fine Handpaints
freiafibers.com

Fyberspates
fyberspates.com

Juniper Moon Farm
knittingfever.com/brand/juniper-moon-farm

Knit Picks
knitpicks.com

Lorna's Laces
lornaslaces.net

Malabrigo Yarns
malabrigoyarn.com

Manos del Uruguay
manosyarns.com

Opal
sandbdistribution.com

Schachenmayr
schachenmayr.com/en

Schoppel Wolle
schoppel-wolle.de/en

Sweet Georgia
sweetgeorgiayarns.com

The Yarn Collective
theyarncollective.com

Acknowledgments

Creating a knitting book is a team project. I'd like to start by thanking my editor, Candi Derr, and the team at Stackpole Books for their trust and confidence in me and for all the hard work they've put into making this book beautiful.

It takes a lot of knitting to produce all the beautiful samples, and I'd like to thank my wonderful team of sample knitters for their hard work and hours of knitting. Thank you to Liz Agnew, Anita Cross, Frances Jago, Jen Snow, Nicky Sutton, and Judy Wilmot. I'd also like to thank all the yarn companies who provided yarn support for this book. I'm so fortunate to be able to work with some beautiful yarns.

Thank you to my husband, Simon, and daughters, Vanessa and Emily, for all their support during my knitting career and for putting up with me while I wrote this book.

My mum taught me to knit when I was a little girl growing up in Norway and helped me to develop my knitting skills during my teenage years. I'm so grateful that she introduced me to knitting at such a young age.

I appreciate support from so many knitters around the world. The feedback I get from you helps me decide what to design next. I love seeing what you knit from my patterns, so do share your projects from this book with me. Reach out to me on social media or join my Facebook group, Love of Lace Knitting.

Visual Index

Milano 23

Benidorm 29

Napoli 33

Palma 38

Malaga 44

Paphos 48

Ayia Napa 53

Madeira 58

Firenze 64

Mykonos   68

Heraklion   72

Crete   77

Ibiza   82

Valencia   87

Monte Carlo   92

Marbella   97

Cannes   103

St. Tropez   110

Barcelona   117

Larnaca   122